LEARNING
BPMN 2.0

A **Practical Guide** for
Today's **Adult Learners**

Visit
proof → 6) Red Rstele
murhity

6) Hecithy tovers MDC — 1) software spec

→ 2) Bielosflow + CALT
active shooter
for tercits
insights

→ 7) promie sele

: 3) option

8) put / aw /cossolt 4) Risk enclyses – non te
cul

Dr. Joshua Fuehrer &
Joseph Butchko

chuck

5) Process anelysis
[Busmer Contih
[Healfy Lme Inspecta

INDIE BOOKS
INTERNATIONAL

Additional Copyrights and Trademark References
PowerPoint® and Visio® are trademarks of Microsoft® Corporation.
Trisotech®

ISBN-10: 1-947480-33-2
ISBN-13: 978-1-947480-33-9
Library of Congress Control Number: 2018958135

Designed by Joni McPherson, mcphersongraphics.com

INDIE BOOKS INTERNATIONAL, LLC
2424 VISTA WAY, SUITE 316
OCEANSIDE, CA 92054
www.indiebooksintl.com

Content

Table of Figures

1. Introduction

Welcome!

1.1 Learning Business Process Modeling and Notation

Do you ever think of how you learn—reading, watching, doing? Maybe you use all three. Many of us go through life unaware of how we learn or acquire a skill set; we just learn it. We all have the capability to learn. It is from that perspective and with a passion for business process modeling with Business Process Modeling and Notation (BPMN) that we set out to write a book that will provide an understanding of BPMN while engaging in the adult learning process for acquiring knowledge.

This book is intended to bridge the gap between theory and practice and make it interesting while we are doing it. While we focus on learning BPMN, we also teach foundational concepts, a balance between academia and real-world examples as it relates to creating knowledge, moving up the spiral of knowledge. With each spiral, more insight is gained, and better understanding is attained.

Wait, what? The creation of knowledge? I thought this book was about BPMN.

Understanding foundational concepts and linking them to real-world examples is the key to our approach. We will provide engaging experiences that create BPMN knowledge. Reading provides one way to obtain knowledge. Practical application, reflective experiences, and collaboration are others sources. We attempt to balance various approaches to enhance your learning experience with BPMN.

A secondary objective of this book is to combine previous research findings in learning with the practical application of BPMN. Specifically, we will provide real-world, practical application of various business process models using BPMN, tips for modeling complex business processes, and strategies that will enable you to capture the knowledge of your organization through business process modeling.

1.1.1 The Concept of This Book

First and foremost, this book is designed to be an experience. It is a collection of tacit and explicit knowledge and a combination of acquired strategies from experts in the field who have years of experience modeling with BPMN. It is based on previous research, anecdotal evidence, and a collection of various resources and videos. The experiences this book provides will help you grasp ideas and transform information in innovative ways, and we hope you will be able to share that knowledge with others in your organization and the broader BPMN community of practitioners.

Secondly, this book explains how you can apply BPMN to your work situation. Specifically, we will demonstrate the most commonly used notations and help you develop better business process models that can have an impact on your organization. This book will cover those notations through an experiential learning approach. We will provide a real-world business process modeling learning experience through an action-and-reflection approach.

1.1.2 What Is (and What Is Not) Covered in This Book

Before we go much further, it is important to cover what and what is not covered in this book. The BPMN specification breaks out three types of models: orchestration, choreography, and conversation.[1]

We will cover the fundamentals required to create well-formed BPMN orchestration models for your organization. Simply stated, we will teach you how to create business process models, from the executive perspective all the way down to the engineering implementation level if you desire. We will take the mystery out of notation, provide clear real-world examples, and put the notation in its proper context.

A conversation diagram is a high-level depiction of how communication (or *conversation*) occurs at a higher level between participants and the processes that connect to each other. Choreography, on the other hand, focuses on the exchange of messages between participants.

We decided to leave conversation and choreography models out of this book, mainly because we see more benefit to the application of the orchestration of business process models with BPMN for our first book. We hope to someday write a second book covering these specific topics. Until then, you can join our discussion on conversation and choreography models on our website. Many of the concepts taught in this book regarding the meaning behind the notations for the orchestration of business process models will have applicability to choreography and conversations.

1.1.3 Introduction from the Authors

We are writing this book from a practitioner's perspective. We started using BPMN as an alternative to the IDEF0 model of process planning and process flow charts when developing enterprise architectures for a large federal government organization. BPMN seemed to cover all the essential ideas—processes, performers, activities, and information flows—all

---

[1] "Business Process Model & Notation (BPMN)." *About the Common Object Request Broker Architecture Specification Version 3.3.* http://www.omg.org/spec

in the same model. We were already capturing the information, and we just needed a better modeling notation to capture it.

Over time, what we came to realize is how easily BPMN can capture robust and complex organizational concepts. We spent a lot of time trying to understand the specification and reading the textbooks already in print. We also came to realize that no matter how much we understood about BPMN, someone else in our community had a different interpretation of the specification. After reviewing the research from the academic community, it became obvious that syntactical errors in BPMN models were rampant in the community of users. Specifically, models analyzed by the research community contained a high percentage of syntactical errors.[2],[3],[4]

So, we set off to study this problem. Josh completed doctoral research on the learning process for BPMN. His research examined the effectiveness of learning theories and the creation of BPMN knowledge from theory to practice. Josh has taken his research findings and developed training material to create meaningful learning experiences to incorporate in organizations—in essence, transferring his knowledge of BPMN to a wide range of stakeholders, modelers, and reviewers to improve business process management initiatives using BPMN.

Joe, acting as a validation and verification agent for the federal government, continued to identify and document misuses and errors in models submitted to the government as contract "deliverables." These models were returned to the vendors for correction and rework, adding cost to the project and causing project timelines to slip. Basic concepts were misunderstood, such as the meaning of a *pool*. He also observed the misuse of the *boundary events*, which resulted in process deadlocks. Feedback to the vendors became learning experiences for vendors to improve upon the application of BPMN.

1.1.4 The Four Knowledge Creation Activities

What we discovered from Josh's research was profound and enlightening. The first thing he discovered was that there was a pattern of activities that look like deeply ingrained assumptions about how experiences are grasped and transformed to create BPMN knowledge.

The following table identifies each of these categories and provides a high-level description (Table 1).

---

[2] Henrick Leopold, Jan Mendling, and Oliver Gunther, "What We Can Learn from Quality Issues of BPMN Models from Industry." IEEE Software. March 2015.

[3] Jan Recker, "Opportunities and Constraints: The Current Struggle with BPMN," *Business Process Management Journal* 16, no. 1 (2010): 181-201.

[4] Suman, R. A., Sajeev, B S., & Ranjan, A. (2014). "An empirical study of error patterns in industrial business process models". *IEEE Transactions on Services Computing*, 7, 140-153. doi:10.1109/TSC.2013.10

CATEGORIES	DESCRIPTION
Applying Concepts	How the creation of knowledge occurred from the practical application of learning experiences.
Exploring Alternate Understanding	How the creation of knowledge occurred from discovering different modeling approaches of learning experiences.
Reflecting on Experiences	How the creation of knowledge occurred from the inductive reasoning of learning experiences.
Analyzing Previous Knowledge Constructs	How the creation of knowledge occurred from comparing existing knowledge with new constructs and deciding what modeling constructs hold true of learning experiences.

Table 1: Experiential Learning Mental Model Categories for BPMN

The four knowledge creation activities depicted in the Experiential Learning Mental Model describe how experiences were transformed into knowledge (Table 1). Specifically, as individuals experienced a new event, they internalized that experience through *apprehension* or *comprehension* and transformed the experience through *extension* (action) or *intention* (reflection).

Oh, more academic terms

The term *apprehension* is used to explain how one grasps knowledge through feelings, senses, and connections. Grasping knowledge through apprehension is *subjective*; we do not know how others feel, think, unless they share their *comprehension* with us.

The term *comprehension* is used to explain how individuals make logical connections between experiences and communicate their understanding of knowledge. In BPMN, it is similar to a colleague explaining his or her interpretation of notations from the specification.

The concepts of *apply concepts, explore alternate understanding, reflect experience*, and *analyze previous knowledge* enable us to provide you with experiences which, when grasped and transformed, create BPMN knowledge. Basically, you will learn BPMN through a series of experiences that will lead to an understanding of BPMN. The better job we do at creating meaningful learning experiences, the greater chance we will have of moving up the spiral of knowledge to form a higher level of understanding of BPMN and reduce the number of syntactical discrepancies in your process models.

Below is a conceptual model depicting how learners' experiences were understood and transformed to create knowledge.

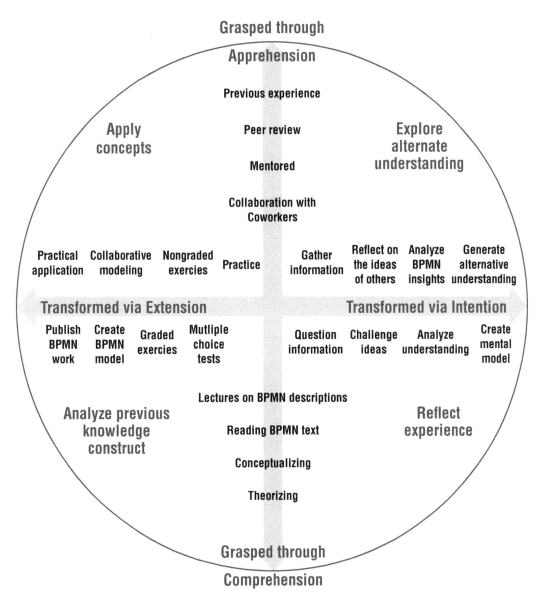

Figure 1: Experiential Learning Mental Model for BPMN

The experiential learning mental model for BPMN describes how experiences are used to create BPMN knowledge. The descriptions in the mental model are not all-encompassing; it is not meant to be a generalized list of all the BPMN modelers of the world.

Rather, it is a framework for applying various grasped experiences to create BPMN knowledge. It enables us to expand on what we know and dive deeper into the learning process and create new ways to learn BPMN. It also enables us to develop meaningful experiential learning experiences.

If we shared only what we know about BPMN, we would fail you, the reader. Our objective is to expand everyone's understanding of BPMN. We intend to create a meaningful connection with you. In this book, we outline how to create a meaningful experiential learning experience. Specifically, we will create a connection through apprehension, because the more you value the source of the experience, the more likely you will be to embrace it. By embracing an apprehended experience, a deeper, more meaningful experience can flow. We also provide you with the framework to create similar experiences throughout your organization.

We hope that through comprehension of all of the provided apprehended experiences, you will form a higher understanding of BPMN, but also, more importantly, how to use BPMN in your organization.

Lastly, we want to teach more than just the BPMN syntax. We are striving for a deeper level of learning. We attempted to design a deeper level of learning through the course of this book through the exercises, personal experiences, videos, and reflection experiences and hope that you become a BPMN practitioner. Our sincere expectation is that through this book, you can develop the capability for modeling with BPMN from a deeper level of learning.

The key takeaway with these conceptual models and framework is that they will become the starting point for you to use as you learn and create meaningful learning experiences in your organization and transfer your BPMN knowledge to others.

As we stated earlier, the experiential learning mental model is not all-encompassing. For experienced BPMN practitioners, we invite you to share insights that could advance this framework and these conceptual models further. To be a part of this exciting research, join our discovery page forum discussion at:

https://www.bpmpractitioners.com/bpmn-forums-and-resources

1.1.5 The BPMN Practitioner's Learning Process

The second thing we found from Josh's research was that each individual has his or her own self-directed learning mental model when learning BPMN. We have individual styles or methods of learning, whether we realize it or not.

The self-directed learner's mental model indicates we work our way through a series of activities during the learning process. This means the individual activities we go through during the learning process influence our understanding of BPMN. The self-directed learner's mental model is made up of five categories (Table 2).

CATEGORIES	DESCRIPTION
Establish Goals	An activity in which personal and professional goals are created that successfully contribute to obtaining BPMN knowledge.
Assess Learning Preference	A self-evaluation of learning style and preferred method of learning when selecting appropriate training and during an engagement in learning.
Identify Resources	A process of finding training material and programs that leads to the type and selection of training materials.
Complete Learning Tasks	A process for carrying out planned learning strategies to acquire BPMN knowledge.
Evaluate Outcomes	The process of validating BPMN understanding from learning experiences.

Table 2: Self-Directed Learner's Mental Model

We can think of these categories as a series of processes, or more importantly, steps in a process. Without knowing how people learned BPMN, we could be missing out on certain critical information.

This became evident during interviews that resulted in the formation of these categories. Specifically, individuals shared how they had struggled to find useful resources that enabled them to learn BPMN. The lack of good resources leads to misinterpretation of the specification, which resulted in poor modeling habits.

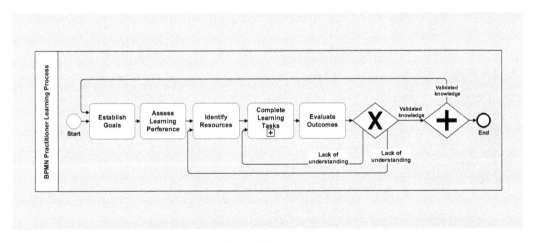

Figure 2: BPMN Practitioner Learning Process

Think of the self-directed learner's mental model as a kind of double loop, or revisiting the material from a different perspective based on feedback, either from validated knowledge or a lack of understanding. While the research did not find an instance of single-loop learning, we posit that there are instances where individuals take a course or read a book and never validate that knowledge against a standard. They merely assume that their models are syntactically correct. Our experience is that individuals become better modelers when they face peer reviews and respond to the feedback—in essence, challenging their assumptions about what they think they know. Learning BPMN favors an iterative learning process.

Through the iterative learning process, we learn and master a concept over time. It also gives us an opportunity to explore the most effective ways to learn BPMN. We hope that you are able to leverage the information, learning exercises, and shared experiences in this book to further advance your understanding of BPMN.

1.1.6 Meet Our BPMN Learners

You have already met one of our BPMN learners. Let's take a moment to explain.

Meditating Mike is always in a deep state of reflection. He is always reflecting on experiences and searching for the reasoning behind everything. When Meditating Mike appears, he provides you an opportunity to pause, breathe, and search within, usually by asking some self-reflection questions, improving your self-reflection skills. As the book progresses, Meditating Mike starts diving into deeper reflection techniques for you to put to use.

General Practitioner is all about action. He is always applying concepts learned throughout life. General Practitioner is always busy, using his energy to apply learned concepts through the action of building a model. When General Practitioner appears, he is reminding you to take action, because without action, what is there for you to reflect on?

Streamer Seth is riding the current wave of technology by offering his own streaming service. He is all about teaching BPMN concepts through his streaming channel. When Streamer Seth appears, he is indicating that there is a corresponding video related to the current topic in which concepts are discussed in additional detail.

BPMN Goal Setters are all about setting learning goals. BPMN Goal Setters have come to the realization that, without establishing and evaluating learning goals, their BPMN skills never truly develop. When BPMN Goal Setters appear, they are reminding you to set a learning goal. Since establishing goals can be challenging to someone new to the field, they do provide sample goals for you to establish and evaluate.

Forum Felicia loves reading the insights of others through blog posts or forum discussions. Forum Felicia is always looking for different perspectives about BPMN. When Forum Felicia appears, she is indicating that there is a great forum post about a specific notation.

Studying Sara loves working out and challenging herself through exercise. She is all about taking her understanding to the next level by assessing what she *thinks* she knows. She has come up with a list of exercises that she thinks will help expand your BPMN understanding. When Studying Sara appears, she is indicating that there are additional exercises in the training folder on our website.

Surfer Dave loves two things: riding waves and providing BPMN pro tips. "Aloha. When I am not catching waves at my favorite spot, I am building sweet business process models. I can teach you how to shred waves or build complex business process models." Since this book is about BPMN, when Surfer Dave appears, he is indicating that he has a pro tip to share. These pro tips are usually for those advanced modelers looking to expand their understanding.

The Inquisitor is always searching for the truth. The Inquisitor may never acquire the knowledge to answer every question, but he pursues the unknown with a passion, always learning new and exciting things, opening his mind to possibilities never before imaginable. When the Inquisitor appears, he is questioning what we, the authors, say, indicating patterns and connections or sharing helpful learning techniques that he has discovered during his adult learning journey.

2. Learning the Basic Categories for BPMN

The intent of this chapter is fourfold.

First, we will discuss why we do business process modeling, and what it entails. Understanding how business process modeling can be used to depict organizational processes is a critical step in transforming the *tacit knowledge* of your organization.

Second, we provide the foundational knowledge to create *business process models* using the five basic categories of BPMN. Application of the basic categories will build the competencies required to understand and apply the advanced modeling concepts introduced later in the book.

Third, we will describe how to incorporate *enterprise fundamentals* into the models of your organization. Our enterprise fundamentals will enable a standardized and consistent look for your models and a way to leverage your *enterprise assets* and reduce the time for business process model development.

Lastly, we will introduce the concept of *systems thinking* and how using a systems-thinking approach will positively influence the BPM initiatives in your organization. Additionally, we describe how you can use the concepts of *enterprise architecture* as a framework for capturing the complexity of any organization.

An overarching goal of this book is to start you down a lifelong path for self-directed learning and provide meaningful experiential learning connections through our interactive approach. We hope that by doing so, we will improve your understanding of BPMN and set the foundation for understanding your enterprise.

Meditating Mike Practiced Reflection

Take a moment and a few slow, deep breaths. As you go to exhale on your last breath, think about yourself within your organization. Do you live and breathe in a small, medium, or large organization? Now envision how you are connected to the members of your organization.

Don't worry if you found this exercise difficult. Without practice, it is hard to see yourself connected to everyone else in your organization. We hope that by the end of this book and through a series of reflective exercises, you will be able to see how processes are connected as well, but more importantly, how the processes are connected to people. These people, with their endless capabilities and tacit experiences, can be harnessed and leveraged to gain a competitive advantage in the marketplace.

We have to confess, being able to see how everyone is connected is only the first step toward implementing a system thinking approach and seeing patterns and interconnected relationships. By practicing reflection skills, you will attain the basic skills for understanding your organization.

One important concept that we find effective in learning is deep, reflective thought. It can be quite rewarding as well as a learning technique. Throughout these chapters, we will provide opportunities to pause and take a moment to reflect on your models and previous experiences or to see the whole organization as a living enterprise filled with potential and capability.

2.1 Business Process Modeling

Business process management aims at solving complex business problems through the creation of models that can lead to innovations that build a competitive advantage, whether it is reorganizing the company, establishing new lines of business, or connecting technology with business strategies.

Just as importantly, business process modeling activities can provide a holistic view of the enterprise by dynamically linking a series of processes to provide employees with a new view of the organization. Through business process modeling, organizations can capture the tacit knowledge of individuals and bring added value to an organization.

Meditating Mike Practiced Reflection

Ask yourself the following: Have you ever started a job and felt lost? As in: "What am I supposed to be doing? What should I know, how do I do that, and what do I do after that?" Have you been in that situation before?

Now think to yourself, how did you make it through that ordeal? Did your organization have a well-documented operating procedure that you could follow step by step? Did someone show you the ropes? If someone did show you the ropes, he or she was actually transferring tacit knowledge of how to get the job done. Was it the best way? Was it the quickest way? Was it the most efficient way? How would you know?

Tacit knowledge (or implicit knowledge) is the secret sauce for *why* and *how* organizations can achieve and maintain a competitive advantage. By documenting activities through business process modeling, organizations are transforming the tacit knowledge of individuals and teams into *explicit knowledge*. The explicit knowledge captured in business process models can be used to align business goals, develop strategy, evaluate performance, drive organizational change, as well as invest in IT, service design, and training, just to name a few.

As we dive into the concepts of business process modeling with BPMN, we will also explore how you can capture the tacit knowledge of your organization. Specifically, we will provide you with the tools and techniques for identifying tacit knowledge that can be captured in your business process models. We will also provide tips and examples of how to transform that organizational knowledge in an explicit form (business process models) that can be leveraged to sustain or gain a competitive advantage.

GOAL SETTER'S CORNER

A goal can be professional or personal.

As we get in the habit of setting very short *educational goals*, we are rewiring our minds into a goal-setting norm. State out loud the following and set these goals:

1. The first goal is to improve my efficiency-building models.

2. The second goal is to improve my understanding of how to use sequence flows, activities, and events.

3. The third goal is to improve how I can visualize the enterprise.

Wait a minute. Did you say those goals out loud?

We understand that to some, stating them out loud may seem silly, but speaking them has a purpose which will reveal itself over the course of this book.

For those who have already achieved these goals, we challenge you to create and set *other* goals. Get into the habit of setting small learning goals. One way to do so is through practical application and reflecting on your experiences. As you learn something new, take a step back and evaluate your understanding. Do you have a complete understanding or a limited understanding? Could you teach the concept to someone else? What goals were you trying to achieve? If you didn't achieve your immediate goals, don't fret! Personal and professional goals should not be viewed in isolation. If you set a goal but do not achieve it completely, it still could be a good learning experience. Goal analysis should not be done in a vacuum, but rather over time as you perform various activities related to your goal.[5]

For those of you who want to identify and track your goals, we have created an online, personalized journal. You can use the journal to identify and define your goals, then record the learning events you tried in order to reach that goal. You can also document your reflections about the whole experience. If you would like to participate and share your experiences as a lifelong learner, please join our forums on goal discussions and we will set you up:

https://www.bpmpractitioners.com/bpmn-forums-and-resources.

---

[5] David A. Kolb, *Experiential Learning: Experience as the Source of Learning and Development,* Upper Saddle River, NJ: Pearson Education, 2015.

2.2 Modeling Inside Your Organization with BPMN

We won't review the full history of BPMN, but it has become the primary tool used in business process modeling. In the following section, we provide a basic overview of business process modeling with BPMN.

The structure of this book is simple. We want to provide an interactive learning experience: one that will improve *apprehension* and *comprehension* through meaningful learning experiences. Through application and reflection, we will engage the cycle of learning by building on your previous knowledge of the business and, using BPMN, express that knowledge clearly. We will make meaningful connections through our discussions, learning exercises, and questions from BPMN practitioners in the field. Additionally, by taking time for reflection, we will be establishing the basic building blocks required to promote deep self-reflection.

2.2.1 Reflecting on What You Do through Business Process Modeling

Customers always ask, "*What can business process modeling do for the organization?*" The answer can take many forms. The following are a couple common examples:

1. Business process modeling enables the evaluation of inputs and outputs of business processes.

2. Business process models enable organizations to capture how the business works in a way that brings value to the various business activities for stakeholders.

3. It creates new opportunities to establish a competitive advantage.

4. It helps create process differentiation.

5. It establishes operating procedures.

From the 10,000-foot level, business process modeling enables decision-making activities as they relate to business process analysis and design, service-oriented architecture, and business process management initiatives. We could literally spend an entire book writing about what business process modeling can do for your organization.

To understand BPMN, you first must realize that it is a *graphical modeling language* with its own specific *syntax* (i.e., the rules behind the language, or *notations*). BPMN is more than just boxes and arrows. It is a means to communicate across different languages and cultures.

Using BPMN, we can describe a basic process flow as a set of *activities*, *gateways* (flow divergence or convergence) and *sequence flows*. Our first example uses only the concepts of events and activities. There will be added features later in the chapter.

The following example shows a cargo management process. The process begins with a *start event* (something that happens during a process, depicted as a circle): in this instance, *cargo arrival notification*. The arrows or sequence flow enables us to connect events and activities as the process continues. The activities *inventory cargo* and *complete cargo paperwork* represent the specific work that is being accomplished. Completion of the last activity constitutes an *end event*. This is an example of a very basic business process.

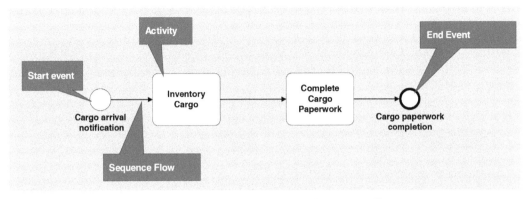

Figure 3: An Examination of a Basic Process Flow

Our team consists of individuals with diverse backgrounds. Our diversity allows us to depict relatable business processes that you would see in many organizations. Again, for us to be effective, we want to make a meaningful connection. We encourage you, as you see examples, to try to model something similar that you know using the concepts demonstrated. We will always provide alternative modeling exercises in the event you want more practice with the concept.

2.2.2 Applying Basic Business Process Model Concepts

Now that we covered the very basics of business process modeling (activities, events, and sequence flows), let's apply these concepts by diving into the underlying application to apply and reflect. To do that, we will use three icons. First, we will we apply our understanding of building a basic process model. Second, we will reinforce this by providing a video link in which you can hear and see us modeling in action. Lastly, we provide a reflection icon to allow you to continue practicing reflection in action.

General Practitioner Application Exercise

Hey! Why are you just sitting there? Let's apply these basic concepts!

Let's transition from reader to business process modeler. To take action, you will need your modeling tool. Open your tool of choice, start a new file, and use the BPMN stencil to do the following:

1. Build your own basic process of what you do for a job. Identify three to five activities, at most, for this exercise. If you don't currently have a job, don't fret. Build a basic process model of what you did today.

2. The key is action. Practice using your modeling tool by dragging and dropping shapes onto the canvas.

   a. Drag a *start event*, then *sequence flow*, and *activity*.

b. Name the first activity (*verb-subject*).

c. Repeat adding a sequence flow after activity.

d. Once you have identified your activities, create an *end event.*

 **Streamer Seth** created a video describing our basic process for managing our educational program. Join us as we build a basic process model of our education program. For those advanced users, you may find some of our other videos more useful.

Join us at https://www.bpmpractitioners.com/videos.

The videos match the figure name. You can also view our YouTube channel, *Joshua Fuehrer.*

Figure 4: Building a Basic Process Flow

The video provides the opportunity to engage through three of your senses (auditory, visual, and kinesthetic). If we were in the physical training environment, we also would turn on our candle warmer and put some jasmine wax to generate excitement and increase the ability of the brain to think. An often-overlooked aspect of engaging all senses is engaging the olfactory (sense of smell). Studies have shown some smells can trigger chemical releases in the brain to promote learning.

Now you have created a basic business process model of what you do or what you did today. Next, close your eyes and think about what you do. Can your job really be depicted in three to five activities? Does your model require a decomposition to truly show the value you bring to the organization? Organizations are generally made up of employees performing roles that contribute to the functions of the organization.

 **Meditating Mike Practiced Reflection**

Try to visualize your organization through a process lens. Close your eyes and try to connect your process with other processes within your organization. Can you see how you fit into the bigger picture?

More importantly, can you see how the processes are intertwined within the organization and how people, resources, and technology come together to produce a product? If you can, is it simple or complex? Can you articulate it in words? Here is where BPMN can help you to visualize and describe the processes of your organization. Before we go off trying to connect all our organization's processes, let's expand the basic knowledge of BPMN.

2.3 The Very Basics of BPMN

The second question customers always ask is, "What is BPMN?"

Business process modeling and notation (BPMN) is a graphical language that enables the development of business process models that are easily understandable. Basically, it is a way to communicate process details using standardized constructs that have a specific meaning. It provides a way for people with diverse backgrounds to understand the process.

Of course, not all people are fluent in BPMN. Organizations that are committed to business process management using BPMN provide tutorials, training aides, and guides to help employees understand the notation. On the other hand, organizations thinking about adopting BPMN may use little more than a marketing flyer. Obviously, some organizations fall somewhere in between the two extremes. Regardless of where your organization is, we hope that the information in this book, our training aides, our resource links to videos, and our forum blogs help you learn and apply BPMN.

2.3.1 The Five Categories of BPMN

BPMN is organized by the graphical aspects of the notation into five specific categories. These are *flow objects*, *data*, *connecting objects*, *swimlanes*, and *artifacts*. The idea behind the categories was to provide the diagram reader easily recognizable elements that lead to understanding the diagram. In this section, we provide a brief overview of each category. Being able to explain how these basic categories work together tends to mitigate the confusion when trying to explain variations in the notation.

2.3.1.1 Flow Objects

Flow objects describe the behavior of a business process model. There are only three types: activities, events, and gateways.

1. *Activities* represent work and describe an action or operation within a business process.

2. *Events* represent something that happens during the process that affects the timing or sequence of the activity or process. Events typically start, end, interrupt, or alter a process. These are called *start events*, *intermediate events*, and *end events*.

3. *Gateways* determine convergence (*joins*) and divergence (*forks*) of sequence flows within a process.

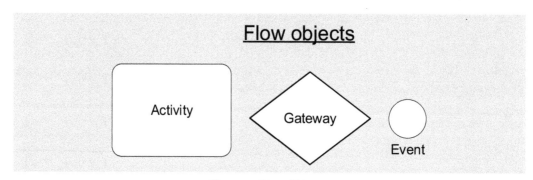

Figure 5: Flow Objects

2.3.1.2 Connecting Objects

Connecting objects are used to link flow objects (activities, gateways, and events) to each other and show information flow within a process. Connecting objects consist of sequence flows, associations, and message flows.

Sequence flows depict the order in which activities occur within a process.

Associations are used to connect information and their associated artifacts with flow objects.

Message flows are used to show how information is passed between two processes or participants (*pools*).

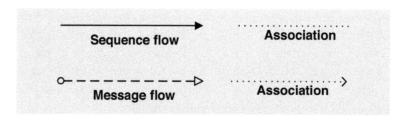

Figure 6: Connecting Objects

2.3.1.3 Data

Data notations are used to describe the instance of information created, modified, or used during the process. Data notations include data objects, data input, data output, and data stores.

1. *Data objects* depict information that is either consumed or produced by an activity.

2. *Data input* depicts the information consumed by the activity.

3. *Data output* depicts the information produced by the activity.

4. *Data store* depicts a mechanism for the activities to retrieve or save persistent information that exists beyond the scope of the process.

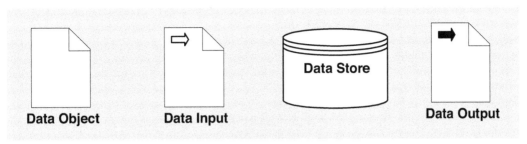

Figure 7: Data

2.3.1.4 Swimlanes

Swimlanes are used to partition activities from one another. There are two types of swimlanes: pools and lanes.

1. *Pools* are containers for partitioning a process (a sequence and flow of activities that carry out work) from other pools/participants (processes). Specifically, they are used to represent participants in collaboration as part of a process. Pools/participants can be organizations, roles within the organization or the process itself.

   - Graphically, pools/participants can be placed horizontally or vertically. (Microsoft Visio will not allow you to create them vertically.)

   - A best practice is to consider a pool as a process (the work being done). This will pay big dividends when depicting complex business processes within your organization.

   - BPMN put out additional guidance regarding the naming of pools and recommends using the participant's name when labeling the pool.

2. *Lanes* are subpartitions within a process/pool. Lanes often represent individual roles (e.g., supervisor, employee, driver, clerk) within the organization.

   - Another best practice is to avoid office symbols as lanes. Office symbols (e.g., organizational branches, departments, etc.) change frequently (are unstable) and will frequently cause your model to go out of date. Organizations love to reorganize; it provides the illusion of innovation and adaptation while often having more to do with internal company concerns. In any event, we consider office symbols to be unstable elements. As such, these should be avoided.

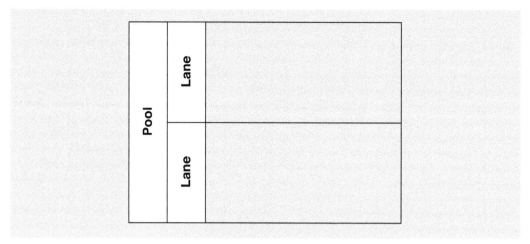

Figure 8: Pool and Swimlanes—Horizontal

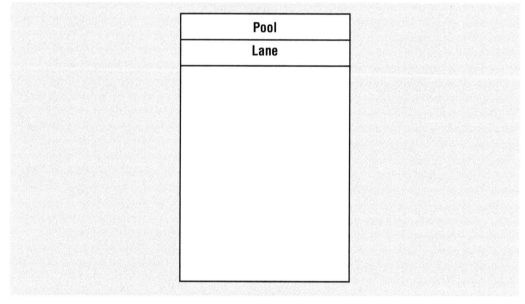

Figure 9: Pool and Swimlanes—Vertical

2.3.1.5 Artifacts

Artifacts are used to convey additional details about the process. Three standard artifacts are the "text annotation," the "group icon," and the "association." BPMN allows for the use of custom artifacts. We will address how to create custom artifacts later in the book. For now, we will discuss the standard artifacts:

1. *Text annotations* enable modelers to provide more details to the process being modeled and are often referred to as call-outs.

2. *Group icons* allow for the grouping of activities, events, and gateways on the model.

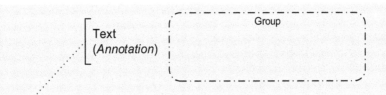

Figure 10: Artifacts

General Practitioner Application Exercise

Let's take it up another notch!

Practice by expanding on your basic business process model. For this exercise, just attempt to recreate the following business process model.

1. Start by creating a pool with two lanes.

   A pool with multiple lanes represents *process orchestration* between the activities, events and gateways and the pool/participants (resources—people, systems, organizations) carrying out the process to achieve an outcome (competitive advantage).

2. As you copy the example, ask yourself: Do you understand the basic notations? As you drag and drop each notation, say them out loud.

   a. Don't forget to label each activity, event, and gateway.

   b. If you don't have these notations mastered yet, don't worry. That's OK. The key is just building this model and restating the notations.

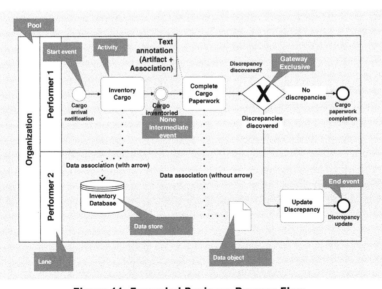

Figure 11: Expanded Business Process Flow

In our example, we depict the five categories describing our basic cargo process. We wanted to show how all the basic categories for BPMN work together when building business process models. This exercise is just another step toward expanding your understanding of how to apply BPMN for your organizational process models.

2.4 Incorporating Enterprise Fundamentals for Modeling with BPMN

In the following section, we provide some enterprise modeling style guides for labeling activities and events for modeling with BPMN. We will introduce the concepts of a central repository to store enterprise *primitives*. We will also provide basic modeling guides that will set the stage for more advanced modeling in chapters 3 and 4. Lastly, we will describe how both systems thinking and enterprise architecture can be used as a tool and a framework for improving your BPM initiatives using BPMN.

2.4.1 Modeling Style Guide

The following is a list of style guidelines. Various authors, practitioners, and bloggers have ideas on the styling guidelines. We typically defer to BPMN's guidance for our styling and adapted the following for our preferred style guide. It is a combination of Object Management Group (OMG) best practices and things that work when applying it to our enterprise architecture efforts.

- *Activities:* Verb-subject agreement for naming (*Complete Paperwork, Create Document, Destroy Obsolete Records*, etc.)

- *Events:* Subject-verb construction for naming (*fire alarm activation, time expiration,* and *buzzer notification*).

There are exceptions to these naming conventions when we deal with timer, escalation, link, error, and compensation events. Regardless of how you label your activities, events, and gateways, the key is to capture and store information about your enterprise.

2.4.2 Central Repository for Primitives

To build a set of enterprise business process models that will link together, you need to use a standard set of participants, processes, activities, events, and gateways. Collectively, we call these elements *primitives*. If you identify and define the primitive the first time you use it and store it, you can reuse it later. This not only provides basic building blocks for your process models but also accelerates the modeling process, because you are not spending the time to define things every time you use them. This concept is not new. The auto industry reuses parts all the time. They design a wheel one time and reuse the design on several different automobile models.

Business process modeling is not all that different from building automobiles, in that it's a repeatable process. Business process models are made up of key primitives (activities, participant, events). We want to leverage these primitives as we build process models. This is where using a central repository is vital for successful business process modeling efforts.

We posit that a central repository is vital for any organization doing enterprise efforts, including architecture, business process management, or model-based systems engineering.

We are huge fans of the research out of the European community. Henrik Leopold, Jan Mendling, and Oliver Gunther reported on quality issues of BPMN models.[6] They provided five key recommendations that we have ingrained in our practice for modeling with BPMN. We highly recommend you read this research as we won't get into all the details in this book, but their fourth recommendation is the use of a central repository that enables reuse and is an *"important requirement for a sound process architecture."*[7] Their recommendations align with John Zachman's view on storing and reusing primitives for successful Enterprise Architecture efforts. By storing and reusing primitives, you are leveraging your enterprise primitives and avoid recreating what you already know.

Many options are available to store and reuse primitives. Many modeling tools allow for library files that can be accessed directly. You could also use database tools such as Microsoft Access and import an extract into a tool. Microsoft Excel is also leveraged as a source for many modeling tools. The key is that you are storing these primitives, the information and details of which can be reused, analyzed, and examined over time.

When process information is properly collected, managed, and stored within your organization, it enables the reuse of enterprise information and provides access to information that can be used to solve complex problems, analyze impacts on business process re-work.

2.4.3 Modeling Conventions

The BPMN version 2 recommends modeling either left to right or top to bottom. This is something we have embraced. We model sequence flows either left to right or top to bottom to improve the readability of our process models.

The following rules apply when using sequence flows and events.

- *Start Events*: Always use an outbound sequence flow arrow.
- *Intermediate Events*: Always have an inbound and outbound sequence flow arrow:
    - Except for *Intermediate Link Events*
    - Except for *Intermediate Compensation Events*
- *End Events*: Always have an inbound arrow.

Events, gateways, and activities (flow objects) are always connected with sequence flows.

---

[6] Henrick Leopold, Jan Mendling, and Oliver Gunther, "What We Can Learn from Quality Issues of BPMN Models from Industry." IEEE Software. March 2015.

[7] Ibid., p.7

 **Streamer Seth** created a video describing inbound and outbound sequence flows from events and activities. This is a foundational video that helps explain basic modeling fundamentals.

Join us at https://www.bpmpractitioners.com/videos.

The videos match the figure name. You can also view our YouTube channel, *Joshua Fuehrer*.

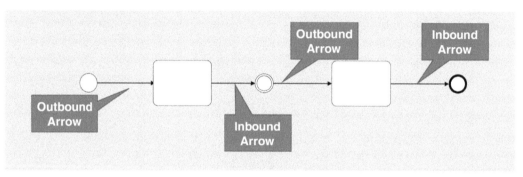

Figure 12: Connecting Flow Objects

After completing the model, fill in the blanks. Practice naming activities and events. Use the verb-subject construction (first the verb, then the noun) for activities, but subject-verb construction (noun first, then verb) for events.

Meditating Mike Reflecting on Action

Ask yourself: Does my activity describe an action? Does my event describe when something happens?

Getting into the habit of reflecting on your actions—in this instance, applying style rules to your process models—allows you to question or view your understanding. Does your understanding align with the material provided? Or did you interpret it in another way? In this book, we hope to challenge your view of a concept through reflection. Doing so enables a validation of knowledge that can lead to higher forms of understanding.

2.4.4 Gateway Fundamentals

A basic modeling fundamental is an interaction between sequence flows and events, activities, and gateways.

1. Gateways determine the branching, forking, merging, and joining of the sequence flows along a process.

2. Gateways control the flow of a process; they are reliant on conditions or business rules associated with the activity before the gateway. Additionally, some gateways are reliant on the events that occur after the gateway. We discuss the differences of gateway types throughout chapters 3 and 4.

3. Gateways are not decisions points. The sequence flow arrows should not be "yes" or "no".

4. Gateways do not represent work.

5. Gateways can be data-based or event-based.

The first gateway we examine is the *exclusive gateway*. The following example depicts the exclusive gateway and how it diverges the process when students are not engaged. The exclusive gateway is data-driven, meaning during the execution of the activity *teach a lesson* an examining of the data *are students engaged* will determine which path we take as an instructor. Are students nodding off? Are they sitting on the edge of their seats, asking questions, and so forth?

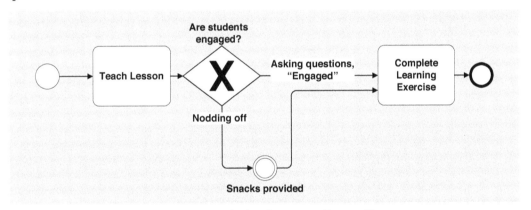

Figure 13: Exclusive Gateway—Engaged?

Do you find yourself engaged? If you answer no, go grab yourself a snack. If yes, let's continue by practicing building a process model with an exclusive gateway. To do this, let's join Streamer Seth who has created a video to help explain basic rules.

Streamer Seth created a video describing inbound and outbound sequence flows from gateways. This is a foundational video that helps explain basic modeling fundamentals using gateways. While watching the video, attempt to follow along while re-creating the same model.

Join us at https://www.bpmpractitioners.com/videos. The videos match the figure name. You can also view our YouTube channel, *Joshua Fuehrer*.

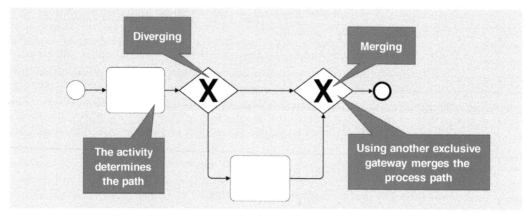

Figure 14: Sequence Flow Example for Exclusive Gateways

Meditating Mike Gateway Reflection

Now let's reflect on your most recent action. Reflecting on action shortly afterwards enables an examination of your understanding of basic concepts.

Ask yourself the following:

1. Take a moment and determine if your diverging gateway has at least two outbound arrows.

2. Does the merging gateway have at least two inbound arrows?

3. Did you use a start and stop event?

Now that we have covered some fundamentals, some modeling conventions, and a brief introduction to gateways, let's discuss some ideas about the enterprise.

2.5 Examination of the Enterprise: A Framework for Capturing Your Process Models

This section describes essential modeling fundamentals that will enable your business process modeling efforts to have far-reaching effects throughout your enterprise. Specifically, we are going to outline some key components for process modeling and how business process modeling fits neatly within the enterprise.

2.5.1 Understanding the Enterprise

Capturing and structuring your enterprise information can be difficult, but it is important. Let's examine why capturing your enterprise information is so important.

Meditating Mike Reflection Corner

Now, let's visualize yourself as a node and visualize the node as a small, blue light.

To do this, close your eyes and count to five.

Node

Figure 15: Node

Pause a moment and countdown from five. Now visualize everyone within your organization as a node. You are surrounded by them. As you try to see these nodes within your organization, start making connections between these nodes based on some sort of interaction (shared process, collaboration, resources, inputs, outputs, or relationships). If you are like us, you can only see so much at first.

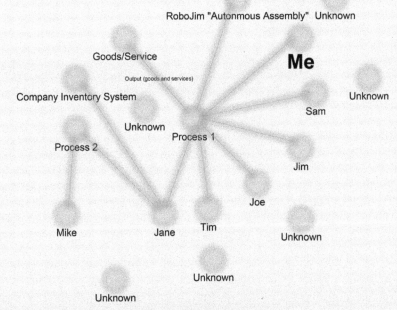

Figure 16: Enterprise Nodes

The enterprise is huge. The enterprise is filled with various departments carrying out activities to achieve a specific outcome: creating or maintaining a competitive advantage.

If you understand your enterprise, you can make well-informed decisions. The *decomposition of enterprise processes* will reveal the transformative nature of your business. Business processes are filled with activities completed by people, machines, systems, and artificial intelligence (AI), that transform inputs (money, customer orders, information, service requests) and generates outputs (goods, services, innovation, tacit knowledge, mental models). Those goods and services are connected to others.

As you begin to identify these patterns, you are developing your own systems thinking process that enables you to see hidden views that, over time, as you build these patterns of these interrelated actions, can enable you to see the whole, or the enterprise.

Wait, what? Systems thinking? I swear you are taking us down the wrong path. I wanted to learn BPMN.

The Inquisitor's response was reactive. If you are like the Inquisitor, always questioning and inquiring, and your response was like the Inquisitor's, that is a prime example of how we view the world today: reactively.

Systems thinking in its simplest form (and we do use the words *simplest form* lightly) is the ability to consider a set of elements interacting with each other to produce a behavior. We consider all the actions within the "system" and understand that those actions have relationships and connection points that influence each other. How those actions influence each other (cause and effect) can either be seen or go unnoticed. Systems thinking can be applied to complex machines such as jetliners, natural ecosystems such as watersheds, large global corporations, or the United States tax code.

Take a moment and ask yourself this: can you see how high-level patterns of change affect every aspect of your organization? Or do you see patterns of change based on what only you can see today? Systems thinking provides a framework for making patterns clearer for us to successfully solve problems that aren't easily seen.[8] A specific example of systems thinking related to this book was from Josh's previous research. Specifically, he identified patterns of how organizations can positively or negatively influence BPM initiatives and learning BPMN. Through the course of this book, we will share those influences plus additional

---

[8] Peter M. Senge, *The Fifth Discipline: The Art and Practice of the Learning Organization* (New York: Doubleday, 1990).

research we have compiled to help your organization promote learning and positively influence change.

We each have our own views or assumptions about how the world works, how our organization operates, or even of our own actions.[9] It is not until we surface those assumptions (or examine those views) that we can truly understand the reasons why we think something or why we react a certain way when we hear something. Surfacing our mental models is critical to understanding a deeper meaning.

2.5.2 Enterprise Architecture

Once you understand that even small organizations involve many interactions occurring both in sequence and simultaneously, you will need a comprehensive framework to study it.

The first step is to identify how you are going to categorize all of those moving parts within your enterprise.

We have leveraged John Zachman's development of enterprise architecture as a framework for capturing the complexity of any organization.

Wait, what is enterprise architecture?

The Zachman Framework for Enterprise Architecture provides a structure for organizations to define enterprise objects (primitives). So as BPMN practitioners, primitives for business process modeling include *roles* (participants), *processes, activities, system functions, information, data,* and *business rules*. Alone, these are just individual descriptions of an *object*.

---

[9] Ibid.

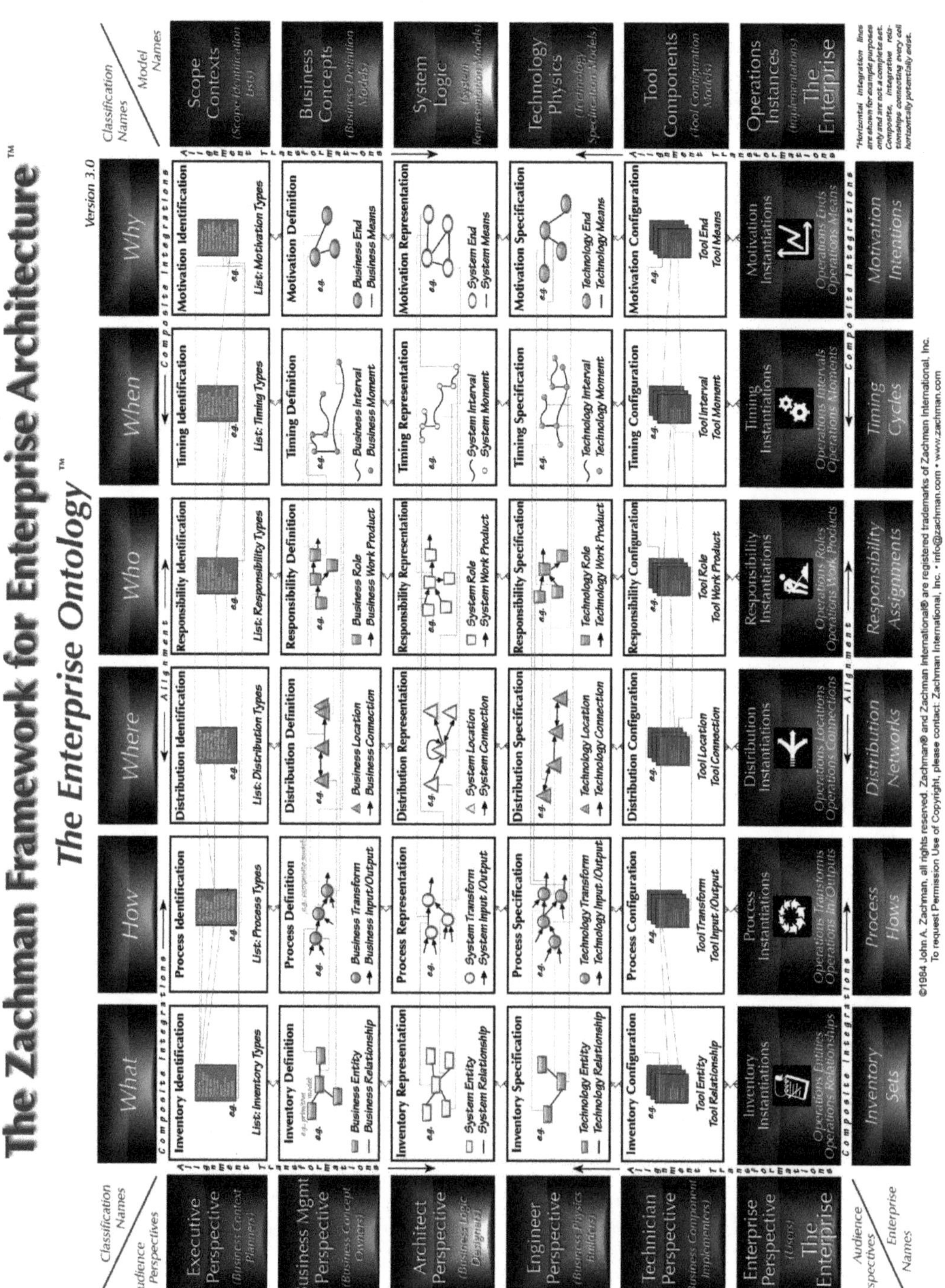

Figure 17: The Zachman Framework for Enterprise Architecture—The Enterprise Ontology

We highly encourage you to work with your enterprise architects, business analysts, or solution-level architects within your organization to define/build enterprise primitives. One of the most useful assets produced from business process modeling sessions are the activities, resources (system, personnel, material), and information which can be stored in an enterprise repository. Great enterprises take this a step further and have found ways to capture personal tacit knowledge of these processes. Tacit knowledge can reveal problem areas, quality issues, improvement ideas, operating procedures, and shortcuts that employees use. More important still are those enterprises which are able to leverage that knowledge to inform policy, make decisions, improve processes, and create and sustain a competitive advantage.

Collaborating with your organization's architects, modelers, and developers will enable the reuse of enterprise primitives when they are captured and stored correctly. When information is captured, it should be cataloged within a repository. Storing and structuring the information enables quick access to various connected resources, either independently as primitive models or within a composite view (a combination of primitive models). As you develop primitive models and composite views of your organization, you will get a sense of the complexity of your organization.

2.6 Closing Thoughts

In this chapter, we introduced a few overarching concepts related to BPMN and process modeling within your organization. If you take anything away from this chapter, it should be that *understanding the interactions within your enterprise is critical*. Doing so will enable you to see how processes, people, and technology are connected, all of which helps visualize how your organization can achieve and maintain a competitive advantage.

This chapter provides guidelines that will enable your organization to succeed in business process management initiatives. By leveraging key concepts such as *enterprise architecture*, *primitive repositories*, and some basic *modeling guidelines*, we hope to set you on the path to improving your BPM efforts in your organization. As we continue throughout this book, we will include some additional modeling techniques and overarching guidance to expand your knowledge.

3. Exploring a Basic Subset of BPMN

3.1 Applying BPMN to Business Process Models

This chapter teaches you how to create BPMN diagrams using the *descriptive conformance subclass notations.*

Whoa! Descriptive conformance *what?*

BPMN separates the notation into three general classes. The *descriptive conformance* typically is used for business process modeling efforts in which processes are not too complicated.

What does this mean to you? Using descriptive conformance class notations, you should be able to create the following business process models:

- High-level, non-executable process models

- As-is business process models

- To-be business process models

- Collaboration between two or more process models

Also, by using the descriptive conformance subclass of notation, you will see a smaller subset of BPMN notations. We have found this enables business analysts to create a business process model that is simple and to show collaboration among key participants.

Additionally, by starting with the descriptive conformance subclass, you can build the basic knowledge needed to transition into more complicated notations (see chapter 4). Since *descriptive conformance subclass* is such a mouthful, we will refer to this as our *basic subset* of BPMN notations.

After you complete this chapter, we highly encourage you to go back to the BPMN specification from the Object Management Group (OMG) and read the section on the different conformance subclasses.[10] It provides additional details regarding the BPMN model elements as well as attributes of those elements. As we move throughout this chapter, we will cover key concepts of the descriptive conformance subclass notation set and also create the knowledge required to move into more complex modeling with BPMN.

---

[10] "Business Process Model & Notation" (BPMN")." *About the Common Object Request Broker Architecture Specification Version 3.3*, www.omg.org/bpmn/index.htm.

3.1.1 Gateways

There are two gateway types commonly used in business process modeling in the basic notation subset covered in this chapter. Each has unique characteristics. The first is the *exclusive* gateway; the second is the *parallel* gateway. BPMN includes several other gateways. For this introduction, however, we will keep it simple and cover just these two.

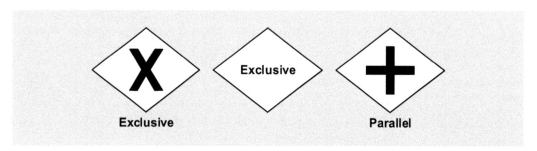

Figure 18: Exclusive and Parallel Gateway

3.1.1.1 Exclusive Gateways

Close your eyes and imagine it is a beautiful sunny day and you are out for a long countryside walk. As you feel the warmth of the sun and a nice breeze, you approach a fork in the road. You have a decision to make. What path do you go down to continue your enjoyable walk? You can only select one path to walk down; you must decide before heading down the path.

A simple trick for conceptualizing exclusive gateways is that exclusive gateways represent a fork in the road, and you can only make one choice. The key to remember is that exclusive gateways do not determine the path you take: the path is decided in the prior activity. In the scenario just described, *you* decided which path to take. The path did not decide *for* you.

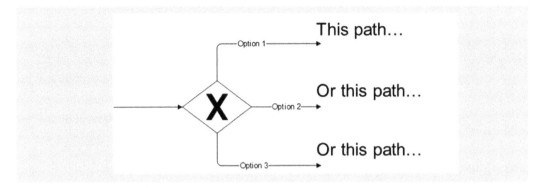

Figure 19: Exclusive Gateway—This Path, This Path, or This Path

As you head down the selected path, you finish out your walk and head home, and the process ends. Exclusive gateways seem simple, right? They are, although the example presented is probably one of the simpler ones you will face.

Now imagine that you wanted to examine the activities you completed on the course of your walk. What if one path presented an obstacle which you moved to clear your way? What if another path featured a little old lady enjoying a picnic who invited you to join? These descriptions are quite interesting and can be modeled for our process.

While we could "end" each path with an end event, what if the process continues or merges at any point? Here, using the exclusive gateway to bring all paths back together makes sense. To bring these paths back together, we use the exclusive gateway to "merge" these paths.

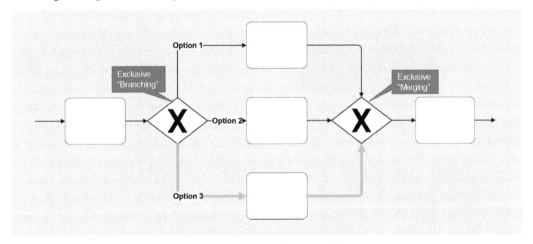

Figure 20: Exclusive Gateway Merge

The following are key characteristics of exclusive gateways:

- Displayed with or without × (but choose one notation and stick with it for the entire model)
- Data-driven, meaning the activity prior determines the path taken based on the response of a question

- Used to create alternate paths within a process
  - Only one path can be taken for a specific instance of the process with exclusive gateways.
- Sequence flows are labeled to identify the condition in which the path would be taken, based on the response to the question
- Require at least two outbound sequence flows from the exclusive gateway
- Require at least two inbound sequence flows for merging exclusive paths

 **Streamer Seth** has created a video for you to follow along while building exclusive gateways.

Join us at https://www.bpmpractitioners.com/videos.

The videos match the figure name. You can also view our YouTube channel, *Joshua Fuehrer.*

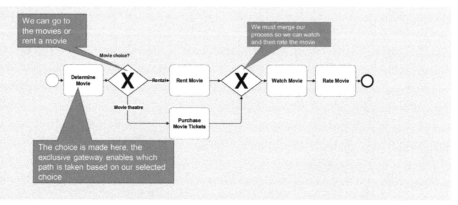

Figure 21: Video Tutorial Example for Exclusive Gateways—Movie Selection

Meditating Mike Exclusive Gateway Reflection

Now let's take a second and reflect on exclusive gateways. Close your eyes and think about your own personal experience at work or in life. Can you recall any decisions you had to make in which you could only choose one path to follow?

A fitting example: A member of our team, Josh, had to decide what to get his doctorate degree in. He is one of those lifelong learners who has a passion for many fields but had to decide one path to take. Thankfully, he chose business management specializing in management education, or we would be waiting for someone else to discover the experiential learning mental model and BPMN practitioner learning process for BPMN practitioners.

General Practitioner Exclusive Gateway Exercise

What decisions do you make? I had to choose between wearing my military outfit or tuxedo for this book.

Let's create a BPMN model using an exclusive gateway.

Take a step back and contemplate your role in the organization. Think about what you do and again, identify three to five activities you complete in a process. But this time, think about when you have to make a choice based on a decision, and model the diverging paths and activities that would follow. Use the exclusive gateway to show the diverging and merging of your process.

For those who are students or struggling to identify a decision in your process, practice building the following cybersecurity process.

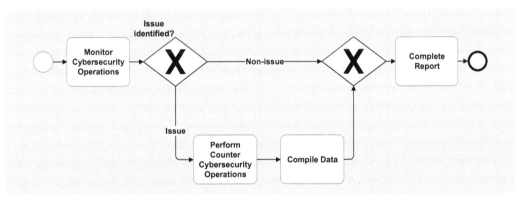

Figure 22: Exclusive Gateway for the Cybersecurity Process

Studying Sara Additional Exercises for Exclusive Gateways

I have additional exercises on exclusive gateways if you are looking to expand your understanding.

Just head to the *BPMN Learning Centre* section in our training folder on our website to complete these exercises and test your knowledge.

The key to remember is that exclusive gateways do not decide which path to take; it is the action (activity) before the gateway that determines the path. It is important to remember this concept because not all gateways follow this convention. In the next section, we will expand on the concept of gateways through an examination of parallel gateways.

3.1.1.2 Parallel Gateway

Where the exclusive gateway enabled you to model a path based on prior actions, the parallel gateway does not require a decision. Parallel gateways sound just like what they do: they create multiple simultaneous activity paths. The use of parallel gateways also enables you to join (synchronize) the process flow after the completion of tasks and events that occur in the process.

The following are key characteristics of parallel gateways:

- Display a plus sign in the diamond

- Use the gateway to create or synchronize parallel process flows

- Generate a *flow token* for each parallel flow occurrence: for example, if two paths are created from a parallel gateway, two tokens will be created, one for each sequence flow. (see chapter 4 for an advanced description of tokens)

- Synchronize parallel process flows by merging the flow with a parallel gateway

- Require at least two outbound sequence flows for creating parallel paths

- Require at least two inbound sequence flows for synchronizing parallel paths

In the following example, we manifest cargo. We use the parallel gateway to create two sequence flows. In parallel, we attach a tracking device and sequence the cargo load (*activities completed*) before loading cargo. No condition or data is needed for parallel gateways. A parallel gateway is also used to join two or more different parallel paths into one path. BPMN calls this *synchronization*. Before the activity load cargo can begin, all paths must be joined.

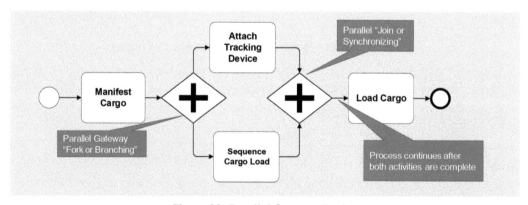

Figure 23: Parallel Gateway Basics

Follow along while **Streamer Seth** creates a business process model regarding a cargo management process using parallel gateways.

Join us at https://www.bpmpractitioners.com/videos. The videos match the figure name. You can also view our YouTube channel, *Joshua Fuehrer.*

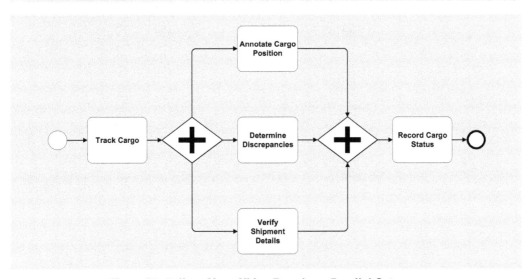

Figure 24: Follow-Along Video Exercise—Parallel Gateways

For us, we live in a state of parallel processes. Specifically, one of our many jobs is the management of architecture being developed. We are constantly evaluating models, evaluating the quality of data, and so forth, in parallel while architecture is being developed. Each of those activities must be completed before we can conduct an architecture assessment.

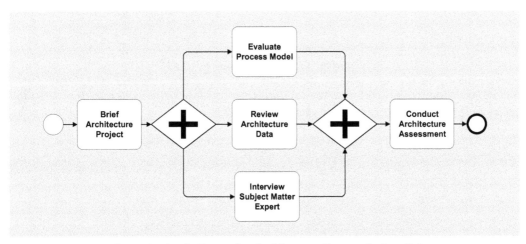

Figure 25: Basic Enterprise Architecture Process in Parallel

Forum Felicia

Introduction to Joining the Forum Discussions with BPMN Practitioners

If you are interested in branch-and-thread concepts, there is an interesting discussion regarding the differences here.

Branch-and-thread is just another way to say diverge, create.

Go to: https://groups.google.com/forum/#!topic/bpmnforum/COOruQ8yl1w

Another example for parallel gateways is the process for training BPMN. In the following model, we depict a simplified process. As students complete training, we evaluate the business process models developed *and* grade the tests to ensure students understand BPMN. However, it is not until both activities are completed that we provide mentorship to students. We wait for both activities to be completed because time is precious and we wouldn't want to mentor students without having a complete assessment from graded tests and the evaluation of their process models.

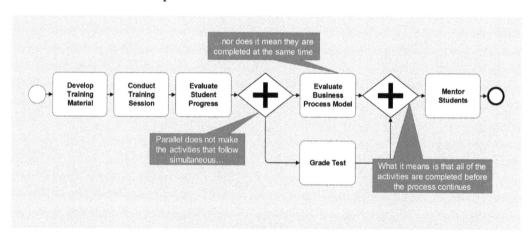

Figure 26: Education Parallel Process

As you examine the parallel gateway and the concept of activities completed in parallel, have you ever conducted a process in parallel at work?

Studying Sara Additional Exercise for Parallel Gateways

Let's test your understanding of parallel gateways.

If you want to test your knowledge on the application of parallel gateways through a multiple-choice test, just head to:

https://www.bpmpractitioners.com/bpmn-exercises

In this section, we described how to use exclusive and parallel gateways. In the next sections, we will expand the use of events. As we dive into events and how to apply them, we will provide additional opportunities to apply the gateway notations discussed here.

3.1.2 Events

Up to this point, we have used events to start and stop a process, but events can be used in other ways. In this section, we dive deeper into modeling with events.

A simplistic overview of events is as follows: *events* represent when something happens in a process.

Events do start or end a process, and they can also occur *within* the process. There are three different general classes of events:

- Start Events
- Intermediate Events
- End Events

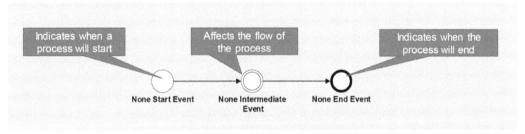

Figure 27: Three Types of Events

Depending on whether it is a start, intermediate, or end event, each has unique characteristics in your business process model. In the following sections, we will discuss each type of event independently and how you can apply these to your process models. Additionally, we will identify and illustrate how you can apply the different event types for these three events.

3.1.2.1 Start Events

It doesn't take long to see that start events are everywhere, from the events that start our daily process, to the start events for making dinner, to the start events that drive our organization's processes. Start events are essential in identifying when a given process will start.

Start events share the following universal characteristics:

- Start events begin the process

- All start events are initiated by triggers from outside the process that are "caught." So, we sometimes refer to start events as *catching events*.

  - Common triggers are *messages, signals, timers,* and *conditions* (e.g., rules such as *sell when stocks hit $50*)

The focus of this section describes three start events (none start event, message start event, and timer start event).

An important concept before we go any further is the *event definition* of each notation. Basically, most events have an event definition that describes the trigger for the event. Event definitions are seen in *start, intermediate, end,* and *throw-and-catch* events. Throughout this chapter, we will cover each of these event definitions as it relates to the specific event type covered.

It is important to note that the event definition for start events describes how the process begins and what specific elements and attributes are associated with that specific event. The following are examples of the three start event types covered in this chapter.

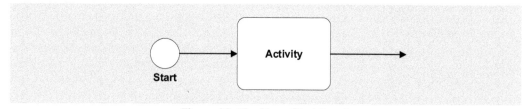

Figure 28: The None Start Event

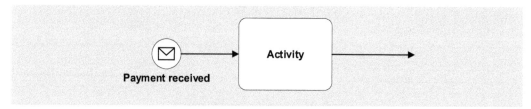

Figure 29: The Message Start Event

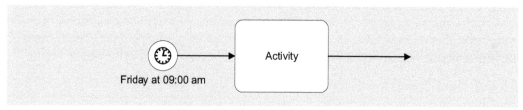

Figure 30: The Timer Start Event

3.1.2.1.1 None Start Events

We provided a basic overview of start event characteristics in the previous section. Now we will dive a little deeper into the *none start event*. Specifically, we want to provide some of the unique characteristics of start events and cover how you can model with them within your organization.

There are three key characteristics of the none start event:

- Can be used for top-level processes or any subprocesses
  - The none start event is useful when first shaping a process.
    - > The process start type may not be clear. Using a none start event avoids trying to determine the specific type of start event to use
- Has no defined trigger;
  - There is no event definition, so the attribute field is blank
- Is displayed with no marker (blank)

General Practitioner Starting the Process Exercise

Hey, start building this model. It's all about practice!

Let's practice building the following model with none start events. Open up your modeling canvas and create the following model. Use a none start event to start our very basic process for creating training material to teach a class.

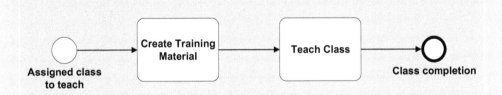

Assigned class to teach → Create Training Material → Teach Class → Class completion

Figure 31: None Start Event

Surfer Dave Pro Tip

Gnarly, dude! The tide is pretty low right now, so while I wait, let me share with you a basic modeling pro tip. Don't forget to label your start event using a subject-verb construction for many of the event types you learn in this book. Of course, there are exceptions to this pro tip, based on your style guide on how to label events.

3.1.2.1.2 Message Start Events

The *message start event* identifies how the process can start with the receipt of messages. The message is received and triggers the start of the process.

The message start event has several characteristics:

- Received from a participant (another pool)
    - *Message* is a concept in BPMN that transfers control of the process (pool/participant) to another process (pool/participant).
    - Messages can be phone calls, faxes, emails, social media notifications, mail, carrier pigeon, or tasking at a staff meeting.
    - Messages can use a message flow (not required).
- Displayed with an envelope marker inside the circle
- Can be used for top-level processes or event subprocesses (described in chapter 4)

Figure 32: Event Subprocess

For the message start event, there is a *message event definition* defined, so we use an envelope to describe when a message is received and starts the process. The *message event definition* is unique to the specific process, as the underlying attributes specify an operation and the message details received from a participant (pool). In the following example, we describe how we receive a message from a social media platform. We use the message flow to depict the information from the social media platform. That notification triggers our process to check out the latest status or photo. We review those new photos and let users know that we like that photo.

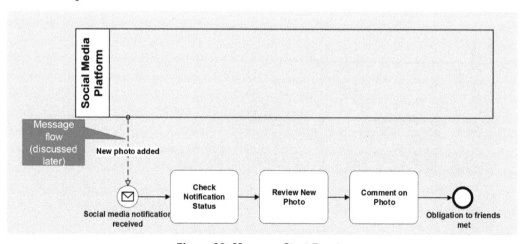

Figure 33: Message Start Events

3.1.2.1.3 Timer Start Event

The *timer start events* are used to specify a time-date or cycle in a process. When using the timer start event, you can articulate specific process times or events that occur around set times.

The timer start event has several characteristics:

- Used for specific time-date or cycles
  - Friday at 10:00 p.m.
  - Every five minutes
  - 2017-07-04 21:00:00
- Displayed with a clock icon
- Can be used for top-level processes or event subprocesses

Organizational processes are filled with timed events. In the following example, we illustrate that the process begins at a set day and time for reviewing security protocols.

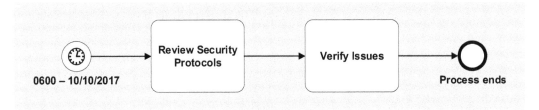

Figure 34: Timer Start Events

It is important to note that the timer start event has a defined *timer event definition*, so we use the clock to describe a specific time and date *or* a specific cycle, and this illustrates when the start event is triggered.

General Practitioner
Time for Another Exercise

Time is the only scarce commodity, so let's make the most of this time to practice three basic models.

Let's test your understanding through the practical application of three start events.

The following are three different processes using each type of start event (*none*, *message*, and *timer*). This is a good opportunity to practice building with start events, particularly if you are new to modeling with BPMN. Open your canvas and recreate the following three processes.

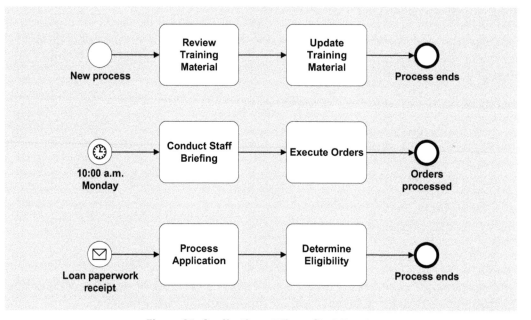

Figure 35: Application of Three Start Events

Meditating Mike
Focused Breathing when Reflecting

After you have completed creating all three processes, take a moment and reflect. Close your eyes and take a few slow deep breaths. Clear your mind.

Now after you have taken those deep breaths, and your mind is clear, reflect on the following:

1. Can you think of other examples of when you received a message that triggered the start of your process at work?

2. What about any time that a specific time or date defined when you began a process?

We promise, as you continue to practice these reflection techniques, you will see the overarching benefits—or have you already? When you reflected on these fundamental questions, could you visualize how these events occur in your previous experiences? Did those previous experiences surface any thoughts or feelings? Our hope is that they did. If not, that is OK: reflection is a lifelong practice that takes time to develop. The point is that we are trying to get you in the habit of practicing various reflection techniques. As we continue our journey in this book, you will have plenty of opportunities to develop these skills to help see things in a new light.

3.1.2.2 End Events

Just as start events are everywhere, so are *end events*. End events tell us when the process is complete. The types of end events add further clarification, as they can illustrate when there is an error or significant issue in a process.

End events share the following characteristics:

- End a completed process
- Represent a result that can be used outside the process. We often refer to end events as *throwing results*.
- Must have a start event
  - A process model does not have to include start and stop events, but we will discuss that later.

This section examines the three types of end events: (none end event, message end event, and terminate end event).

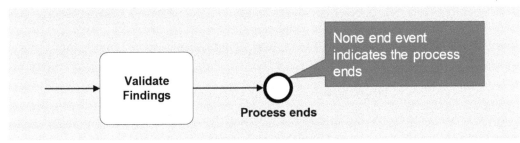

Figure 36: None End Event

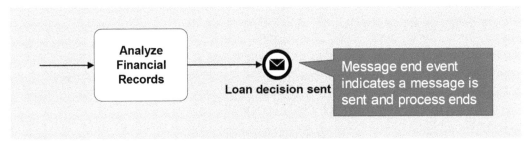

Figure 37: Message End Event

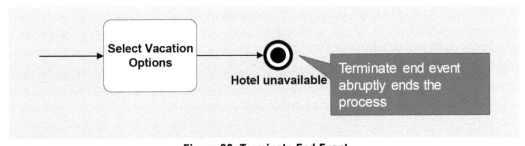

Figure 38: Terminate End Event

3.1.2.2.1 None End Event

None end events are used when the end of the process has no associated event definition. This means as modelers, we can use the none end event when the process ends with no specific action defined.

None end events share the following characteristics:

- Do not have an event definition

- Displayed without a marker

In the following example, we demonstrate how to use the none end event.

As we receive a payment, we check out a bank statement. After we have checked to make sure we were paid for our services, the process ends.

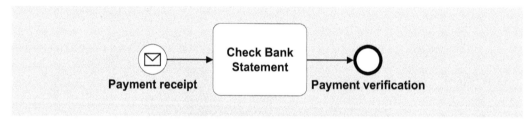

Figure 39: None End Event—Payment Verified

If the process required us to notify the sender that we received payment, how could we model it? In the next section, we discuss how message end events can be used for sending messages at the end of our processes.

3.1.2.2.2 Message End Events

We use *message end events* in some form in many of our processes. Message end events are a convenient way to communicate information that is being sent at the end of our process. Have you ever completed a set of activities in your job in which you had to send an invoice, notify a customer, or email information to a coworker?

Message end events share the following characteristics:

- Messages are sent to a participant when the process ends.

  - Option to use a *message flow* to connect to the participant.

- Messages are used to communicate in a process.

  - Just like message start events, message end events can be emails, faxes, phone calls, and social media notifications (or *none electronic* means messages such as hand delivery or talking to someone).

In the previous section, we used the none end event to indicate that we verified our payment. But what if we wanted to send a payment confirmation email to the customer? The message end event enables you to communicate that information. In the following example, we depict a simple example of the message end event describing such a process.

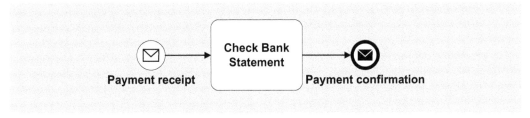

Figure 40: Message End Event—Payment Confirmation

We see all sorts of uses for message end events. In the following example, we depict a simple cargo arrival process. As cargo is received, cargo is stored, and the customer is notified. A message end event is used to communicate cargo arrival details to a customer. The key to remember is that all end events are *throwing events*, meaning the process transformation that occurs is communicated by the information *thrown* from the process.

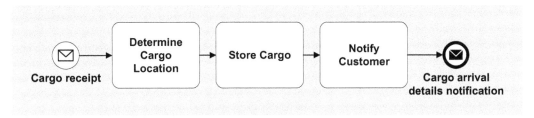

Figure 41: Message End Event—Communicating Cargo Arrival Details

3.1.2.2.3 Terminate End Event

Terminate end events abort the entire process instantiation. These events allow us to model what happens when a process is stopped prematurely.

Terminate end events share the following characteristics:

- Cause the entire process to be aborted
    - Includes any remaining active activities
- Displayed with a dark circle within the end event
- Can be used for any type of process

In the following example, we describe something we all love to do: car shopping! (*Go ahead and insert sarcasm if you haven't already.*)

So, you have found that perfect car, but while you are selecting all your car package options, the dealer is having you fill out loan paperwork and is negotiating a price. But then the worst happens: you are denied the loan. If the loan is not approved, the process ends, and any activities cease. Without the money from the loan, you cannot purchase a car.

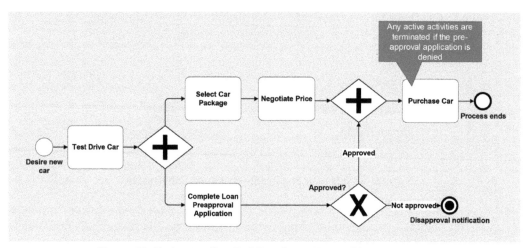

Figure 42: Understanding End Terminate Events Characteristics

For the terminate end event, there is a defined *terminate event definition*, so we use the terminate end event to abruptly end the process. For example, if we were planning a vacation and searching for hotels and flights, we may be able to find a flight that fits our schedule, but we are unable to find the hotel. Thus, the use of the terminate end event would abnormally terminate the entire process.

General Practitioner
Applying Terminate End Events Experience

Let's take action and apply the terminate end event to the following exercise.

Let's practice by modeling with terminate events. For this exercise, let's keep it simple and recreate the following model about determining our next vacation.

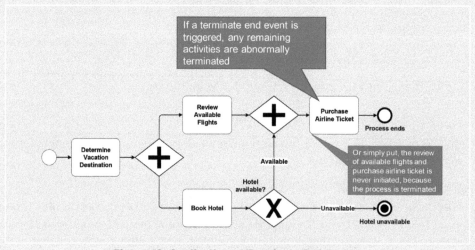

Figure 43: Application of Terminate End Events

My family has selected our vacation destination—Hawaii. So, we need to book a flight and a hotel. We split up the work. My wife is booking the flight, and I am booking the hotel—a parallel process. What happens if all the hotels are booked, and there are no rooms available? If a hotel room is unavailable, I tell my wife there are no rooms, and she stops looking for a flight. We can model this by using the exclusive gateway to depict the results from "book hotel." In this instance, the hotel is either available or unavailable. We then use a sequence flow from the exclusive gateway to a terminate end event. The terminate end event will stop any ongoing activity, such as booking the flight, and none of the follow-on activities will be initiated, such as purchasing the tickets. That is the significance of terminate end events.

These application exercises that appear early in our book are more about recreating some sort of model with an accompanying narrative. As we progress through the book, we move from these types of application exercises into *more complex exercises* requiring you to analyze narrative text or use-case information to apply your knowledge of BPMN. For those BPMN practitioners who have an advanced understanding of a notation discussed, we challenge you to take these building block exercises to the next level and put your own spin on creating a narrative to build a custom model using the notations discussed. After you have completed your narrative and model, we encourage you to share it on our website and discuss.

Meditating Mike
Recall Doodling Technique for Reflecting on Experience

Take a piece of paper or whiteboard and slowly draw a circle. When the point of the pen or marker meets to connect the circle, keep going in circles with your pen/marker. Keep drawing (doodling) the same circle for a couple minutes. During this process, just solely focus on drawing the circle and clear your mind.

Now, let's reflect on any previous experience related to terminate events. Ask yourself, does something abnormally occur in your process that terminates other actions completed by you or others? The technique of structured doodling has been shown to improve individual ability to recall memories.[11] So, practice this technique when you feel stuck or have a need to recall previous experiences.

---

[11] Jason Bruce Boggs, Jillian Lane Cohen, and Gwen C. Marchand, "The Effects of Doodling on Recall Ability." *Psychological Thought.* March 31, 2017.

3.1.2.3 Intermediate Events

Intermediate events enable you to model when something happens (a *trigger* is *caught* or *thrown*) within the process. Whereas start and end events have a specific purpose for starting and ending the process, intermediate events occur *throughout* the process, and they affect the flow of a process model.

Intermediate events share the following characteristics:

- Indicate where something happens in the process (a trigger is caught or thrown)

- Can be catching and throwing control of the process to another pool/participant

- Will not begin or directly end a process

- Can be placed on the *boundary* of an activity (discussed in chapter 4)

In the following example, we describe a basic shopping process. Our hunger triggers the process. The first task we complete is to compile a shopping list. Before we can prepare dinner, however, we must go shopping. As we complete our shopping, we notice a blue light special. The deal is so great that it affects our process; we buy additional items because of the low price. We use the none intermediate event to illustrate that the event *blue light special* has affected our process flow. Once that event occurs, our process continues, and we buy the additional sale items. We can then prepare dinner.

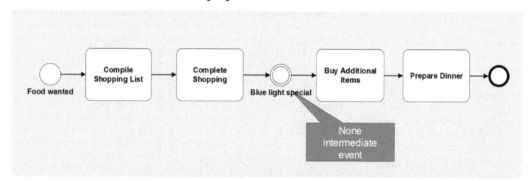

Figure 44: None Intermediate Event

You can think of intermediate events when you model your organization as a way to depict when something occurs during the process. Does your process have to wait for a specific time to continue, or does it have to wait to receive an email or message to continue or something to be sent? Throughout this section, we describe a few different intermediate event types and illustrate the practical application for modeling these event types in your business process models.

3.1.2.3.1 None Intermediate Events

We will briefly cover the *none intermediate event* in this section. Similarly to the none start event, none intermediate events do not have an event definition. While the none intermediate event is useful for modeling early on during the development of the **first iterations of our process model**, we typically find other intermediate event types more meaningful and tend to gravitate toward using them. The main reason is that other event types have event definitions that help us define the trigger (or what's occurring). It is a great way to communicate organization process events to multiple stakeholders.

None intermediate events share the following characteristics:

- Does not have an event definition (just as the none start event)

- Can be used only during the *normal flow* (cannot be on the *boundary* of activity)

- Displayed without a marker

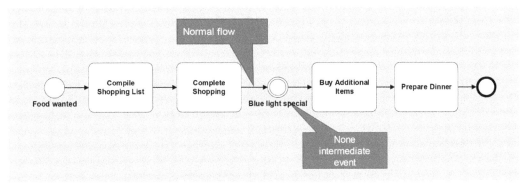

Figure 45: Examination of the None Intermediate Event

A side note for those who have seen boundary events or modeled with them before: we will discuss boundary events and the application of events on the boundary of activities in chapter 4.

Let's continue the examination of intermediate events and model out a simple household process: something most of us should have experience with—doing chores.

General Practitioner
Application of None Intermediate Events

Wait for a second, doing chores is not fun! I want to build BPMN models. Oh, well. Let's combine both.

Instead of doing chores, we will use BPMN to model out our chore process using intermediate events *and* parallel gateways.

- Our process begins, and the first activity of our chore process is to *complete general cleanup.*

- Use the parallel gateway to depict two paths.

  - One path taken leads to the second activity of our chore process: *dust living room.*

> Upon completion of dusting the living room, a sequence flow leads to a parallel gateway (synchronization).

– The second path taken leads to our third activity: wash clothes.

> Upon completion of washing the clothes, a sequence flow leads to a *none intermediate event* to illustrate that the washer cycle has completed.

o By using the *none intermediate event*, we are signifying that the process cannot continue until the event *washer cycle is completed* occurs.

– The fourth activity after the none intermediate event is *unloaded washer*.

– The fifth activity after *unload washer* is *fold laundry*.

> Upon completion of folding the laundry, a sequence flow leads to the parallel gateway (synchronization).

• After we have completed all of our activities, a sequence flow leads from the parallel gateway (synchronization) to an end event.

– Remember that for the process to continue with a parallel gateway, all active activities and paths taken must be completed before we can continue our process

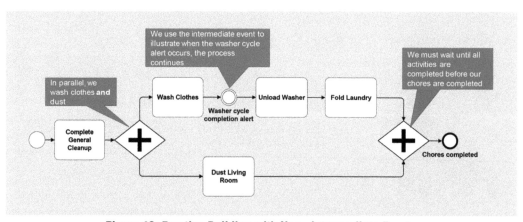

Figure 46: Practice Building with None Intermediate Events

We use the intermediate event to control the flow of the process to illustrate that this event must occur before we can fold laundry. As we dive into intermediate events, we will illustrate the power of controlling the flow of the process based on events, or the things that occur.

Surfer Dave Pro Tip

Bro, teaching bad concepts is like teaching bad form for surfing: it will come back to haunt you! The previous examples of none intermediate events are great for teaching the concept, and like the authors stated, none intermediate events are great for TBD or placeholders until you have enough details to figure out the event types.

The following would be a more accurate way to represent the event types. We will get into why *signal events* would be a better fit here in chapter 4; but basically, signal events are used when there is not a specific target, but rather a general notification which affects the process flow.

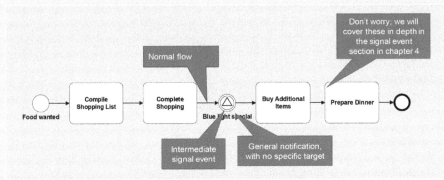

Figure 47: Surfer Dave Pro Tip—Correct Event Types—Blue Light Special

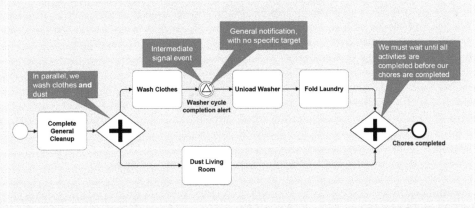

Figure 48: Surfer Dave Pro Tip—Correct Event Types—Washer Cycle Completion Alert

3.1.2.3.2 Message Intermediate Event

Message events can be emails, faxes, phone calls, social media notifications, by carrier pigeon or nonelectronic, such as letters or talking to someone. *Message intermediate events* share the following characteristics:

- Used to communicate in a process

- *Throwing* messages are displayed with a dark filled-in envelope

- *Catching* messages are displayed as an unfilled-in envelope

Message intermediate events, just like *none intermediate events*, are used to model out when *something occurs* during the process—in this case, when a message is received or sent. As teachers, we typically create our training material in advance of holding class. It is between creating the training material and class when a lot of things occur in our process. We can use the message intermediate event to describe how, upon receipt or *catch* of the student list from an organization, we are able to prepare for class by ensuring we have resources for the appropriate number of students. In the following example, we illustrate the *catch* concept. We can create all the training material in the world, but until the *occurrence* of receiving that student list, our process doesn't continue.

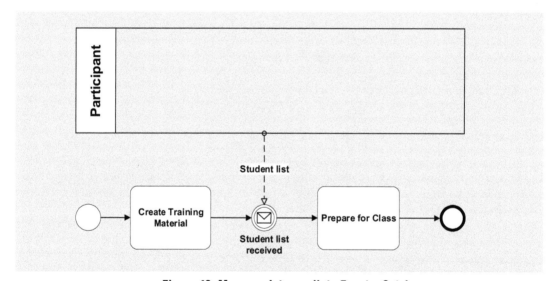

Figure 49: Message Intermediate Event—Catch

Let's expand on the *catch* concept by including the *throw*. In the following example, we use a message throw and a message catch during the normal process flow between two activities. After a report is created, we use the message throw, illustrated with the filled-in envelope, to show that we send a report to an actual pool/participant (not shown). We then use the message catch from the pool/participant to describe that our processes don't continue until discrepancies are received. Basically, our process sits and waits for the intermediate message catch event until the event *discrepancies received* occurs. Once we receive discrepancies, the process flow continues, and we can modify the report.

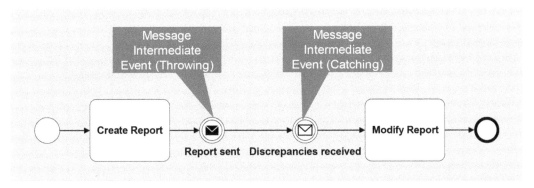

Figure 50: Message Intermediate Events—Throwing and Catching Concept

The application of the *throw* and *catch* intermediate message event enables you to show the flow of information in collaboration. Additionally, throwing and catching enables you to show how process control is changed. If an intermediate message event is depicted as a throw event, then as soon as that event occurs, a message is sent; you are passing control to a participant outside of your process. As soon as a message *throw* occurs, the process then waits to receive *catch* information from the participant outside of your process.

In the following example, a *test* is sent to the student. Control is passed to the student because he or she must complete the test. Our process flow moves to the intermediate message event *catch,* and the process will wait until the student sends *test results*. Once test results are received, the process flow will continue, and we can *evaluate* test results. In this case, control of the process is transferred with the message throw. The control of the process is now with the student. Until the student returns the test, the original process is in the *wait* condition.

If we could connect with the student and the student can grasp the concept of throw and catch, then no updates should be required to our training material. "Why is that?" you ask. Because after we receive the test results, we will evaluate them. We use the exclusive gateway to depict that there are two options based on our evaluation. If the data indicates that students didn't grasp the throw and catch concept, we will update our training material, because we failed to make that connection. However, if everyone understands this concept, then we can proceed, and the process ends.

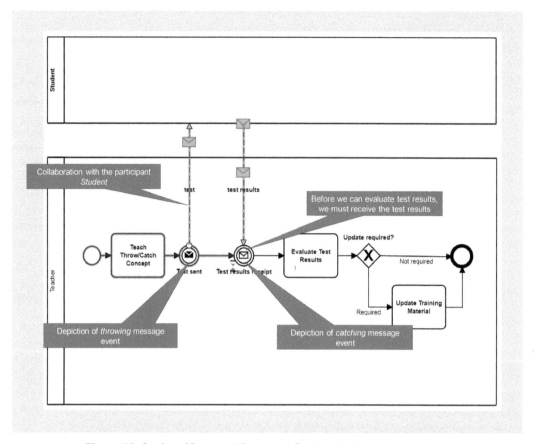

Figure 51: Analyze Message Throw and Catch with Trisotech Modeler

In the previous example, we use the animation feature of Trisotech to illustrate the throw and catch, or how the message (*envelope*) moves through the process. In essence, we are throwing control to the student, because we cannot continue without receiving test results.

General Practitioner

Create BPMN Model with Throw and Catch Message Intermediate Events

Wait, why wasn't carrier pigeons used as a method for throwing and catching in that last example? Oh, well. I guess with technology, some things become obsolete.

Let's take a moment and practice building the following model. The key here is to apply the concept of intermediate message events for this basic process.

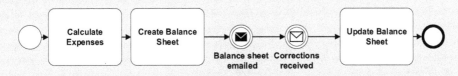

Figure 52: Developing a Process Model with Intermediate Message Events

For advanced users, add a parallel gateway with an additional throw and catch message and two participants describing a process you are familiar with. When you are done, feel free to join the conversation on our forum discussion and share your process.

Meditating Mike Reflecting on Stuck Processes

Look at the previous model closely and ask, how long would you wait to receive corrections before moving onto the activity "update balance sheet"?

The answer: indefinitely. The way the model is depicted, we must wait on receiving corrections before continuing. However, as modelers, we have options to avoid getting stuck in our process. We will cover this a bit more as we continue to peel back the layers of BPMN.

3.1.2.3.3 Timer Intermediate Event

Like the timer start event that we previously discussed, the *timer intermediate event* shares similar characteristics. The timer intermediate event is also a *catching event* and is used to indicate a specific time-date or cycle. The difference with the intermediate event is that it acts as a *delay mechanism* in the process. We will discuss important characteristics of the timer intermediate event and how you can apply it to your process models.

Timer intermediate event shares the following characteristics:

- Acts as a delay mechanism within the process flow

  - Used for specific time-date or cycles

  - Displayed with a clock icon

- Are *catching only*

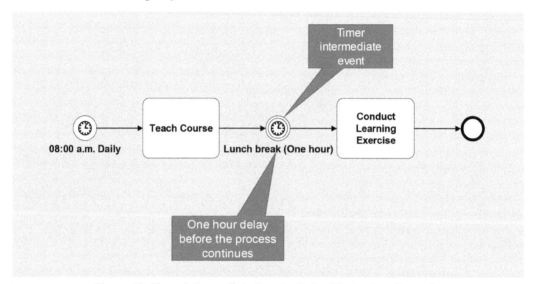

Figure 53: Timer Intermediate Event—Delay Mechanism Example

Organizations care that their processes lead to a competitive advantage. *Timer events* are quite useful when modeling out organizational processes, specifically when there are time delays or cycles relevant to providing a good or service.

In the following example, we show a standard automotive repair shop process using timer events. The process is pretty simple: It begins at 7:00 a.m. daily at the beginning of a shift. The shop goes through a series of activities for repairing a vehicle.

We use the *timer intermediate event* to illustrate that after arranging for a vehicle repair, they wait two hours (*cycle time*) before the process continues.

It may be relevant to an organization to capture the fact that it takes two hours before a customer may pick up a vehicle. Could they improve customer satisfaction by decreasing the wait time? Or does the process already have an optimal benchmarked time? Until you capture specific time events that occur during the process, you may never know.

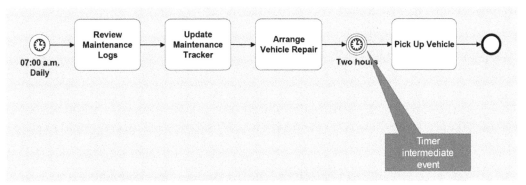

Figure 54: Timer Intermediate Event Explained—Repair Process

Meditating Mike Taking Time for Reflection

Time for reflection is everything, even for the simplest problem. How long would the intermediate timer event delay the previous process?

The answer: two hours. While this was a simple example, now imagine having five timer intermediate events with various times, gateway paths, and so forth. Understanding the control flow and which timer is enabled will allow you to analyze process information as you start building out business process models.

General Practitioner
Conceptualizing a Process without Activities

The point of a process is to show the transformation. But it's fun to break the norm when learning.

Let's visualize our process model without activities. To do this, we are going to have a little fun with intermediate events and apply what we have learned so far. *Without looking* at the provided solution, create a process model without activities.

- Create a process model based on *events*.
- Engage in creative thought to build a process model with a start event, intermediate events, and end events.
- Use parallel gateways (fork and synchronize).
- As you place each notation, *state out loud* which notation you are using.

After you complete your model, take a look at our following example. Was your model different? If so, we would love if you shared your example on the forums.

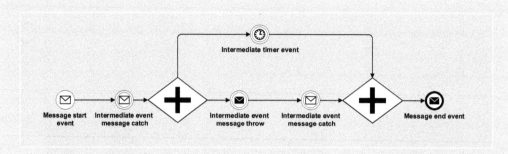

Figure 55: Conceptualize the World Without Activities—Fun Times with Events

Did you know that listening to classical music helps enhance spatial-temporal reasoning?

Spatial-temporal reasoning enables us to visualize patterns and how to arrange objects. When learning and applying BPMN, improving our spatial-temporal reasoning would, in theory, improve how we can see how processes are connected, how to arrange the notations based on our knowledge of BPMN, and how we can visualize the patterns.

We recommend when you are in the mood and are building a model, to listen to classical music. We all vary in our preferred music, but some of our favorites include Mozart, Vivaldi, Handel, Bach, and Telemann.

This section provided a baseline of events that you can use to start applying to your business process models. These basic event types are the key to any good business process model. They are commonly used in the development of business process models and enable us to dive deeper into other event types in chapter 4.

But before you move on to solving your organization's problems with BPMN, let's expand your understanding of modeling with activities and tasks in the next section.

3.1.3 Modeling with Activities and Tasks

Thus far, we have used a *task* object as a basic way to describe an *activity* within a process flow. Activities are used to describe work an organization completes in a process. Now we will dive deeper into activities by explaining the differences in the activity notation and how you can apply them to your process models effectively.

Tasks are *atomic*, meaning they cannot be broken down into any finer level of details. In this section, we will describe four BPMN tasks. In chapter 4, we will describe the remaining task types, but for now, let's illustrate the following task types:

- Manual task
- User task
- Service task
- Call activity

Figure 56: Manual, User, Service Task, and Call Activity

This section provided a basic illustration of the activities and tasks required for basic BPMN models. We will now dive into each type of task and activity in the following sections and demonstrate how you can apply these to your business process models.

3.1.3.1 Manual Tasks

Out of all the notations, modeling with *manual tasks* is probably the most stimulating notation.

Wait, what? Did you really just say stimulating notation?

We did. Because if you look at manual tasks as opportunities to improve current as-is processes, organizations are filled with manual tasks. To us, that is exciting.

Think of the manual task as something that is completed without the assistance of a system or any form of automation. Organizations are cluttered with manual tasks and processes. How many times have you completed a manual task? Now, ask yourself how many times you have thought that a manual task could be automated.

Identifying manual tasks gives you an opportunity to identify mundane tasks that can be automated.

The following are characteristics of manual tasks:

- Identified with a hand in the upper-left corner of the box
- Completed without the assistance of automation

In the following example, we illustrate a basic manual process for cargo management for building cargo pallets. We illustrate three manual tasks. Each manual task (illustrated with the hand in the upper-left corner) represents work done without automation by employees performing a series of activities with their mind and might.

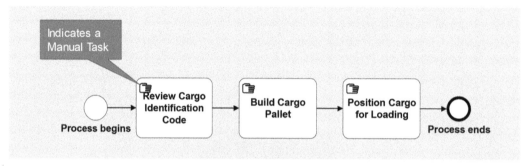

Figure 57: Manual Tasks

 **Streamer Seth** has created another video if you want to learn more about manual tasks. Follow along while we build a process for teaching BPMN using manual tasks.

Join us at https://www.bpmpractitioners.com/videos. The videos match the figure name. You can also view our YouTube channel, *Joshua Fuehrer*.

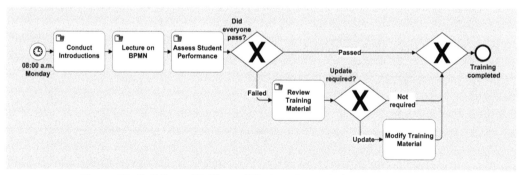

Figure 58: Building with Manual Tasks—Expanded Training Example

General Practitioner
Building with Manual Tasks

Let's manually create a model using a piece of paper or whiteboard.

Think about manual tasks that you have performed at work in the past and create a model with manual tasks you perform without the assistance of a tool. Use a whiteboard or piece of paper.

1. Create a process with manual tasks

2. Ask yourself, would you or could you automate any of those manual tasks?

3. After you create the model, take a picture with your phone or camera and add it to our forum discussion on manual tasks

Meditating Mike
Feeling the Pressure

Let's role-play a bit. Imagine you oversee your organization for the day, and you have the authority to move mountains regarding change.

Take a moment, think about processes you are familiar with, and ask yourself the following:

1. Would you automate any of the tasks you identified?

2. Do you know what would be a good *quantifier* to automate tasks?

Before you answer these questions, some things to think about are:

1. Is the task repetitive or mundane?

2. Can the task be automated cost effectively?

Identifying manual tasks is only part of the battle in understanding whether your processes are competitive. Understanding costs to automate, resources required to complete a manual task, and the output of manual tasks are essential considerations for competitive processes.

3.1.3.2 User Tasks

The second type of task that we are going to cover in this chapter is the *user task*. A user task is performed with the assistance of an application or system. We also include *equipment* in this category. Organizations are made up of employees utilizing software and applications to complete their work.

Think of the user task as someone completing work using a software application such as Microsoft Excel to verify account balances or a system that helps you process payments. The following are characteristics of user tasks:

- Identified with a person icon in the upper-left corner
- Completed with the support of an application or system

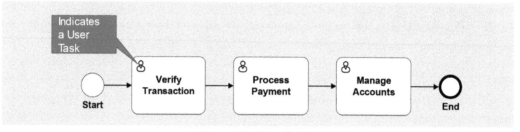

Figure 59: User Tasks

General Practitioner
Building a Process Model with Manual and User Tasks

Don't let the fear of not knowing keep you from the action. Practice makes perfect. The practical application of modeling enables trial and error.

Let's apply your understanding of manual and user tasks and recreate the following business process model for system change requests. As you are building the model, a key takeaway is the identification of the task types you use.

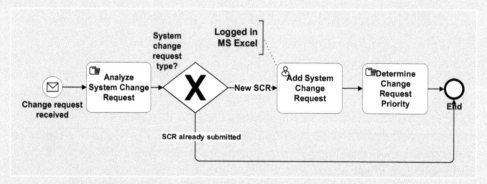

Figure 60: Applying User Tasks to System Change Request Process

The user task shows that we use Microsoft Excel to track all system change requests. Showing this adds value to an organization trying to improve its process because it leads to the question: Have you ever tried using a tool like Serena? While we love MS Excel, there is a time and a place for using it. Managing system change requests, in our opinion, is not one of them.

Studying Sara
Use Case for Identifying User Tasks

Do you want to improve your identification of user tasks? There is an exercise that will provide some real-world examples of identifying user tasks.

The key is to experience what analysts go through. Take a moment and test your analysis skills. We encourage you to complete this exercise with a group of colleagues who also use BPMN. We find this type of collaboration can help surface new understanding.

Download the use case from our training folder on our website and share with your colleagues: https://www.bpmpractitioners.com/bpmn-exercises

If you are reading this on your own, no worries; you can post on the forums, and we would be glad to discuss your analysis.

Before we move on, are you starting to see a pattern emerge yet? Do you see that your organization's processes are made up of distinct types of tasks? As we continue to dive into BPMN, patterns should start to emerge that represent how your organization functions. Understanding the task types will enable a clear representation of how activities are being completed. In the next section, we describe the service task and how you can apply it to your business process models.

3.1.3.3 Service Tasks

The third task we will discuss is the *service task*. This is a task that uses a service, which is either triggered by an application or web service. Can you think of any service tasks in your organization? The following are characteristics of service tasks:

- Identified with a gear in the upper-left corner

- Invoked by an operation
  - To be invoked by an operation, the message into the service task must have an item definition.
  - See the **Surfer Dave Pro Tip** below for an expanded description of operation.

- Represents a service request/response [think web services]

- Can be used to identify business logic error or conditions that were not expected or experienced: a *fault* is returned, and an interrupting error event occurs (see chapter 4)

Our organization uses specialized security software for monitoring threats to our systems. In the following example, we model out the basic process for threat management. We use the service task to illustrate how our system detects threats and the steps taken when a threat is detected. You will notice we do not have any manual or user tasks in this process.

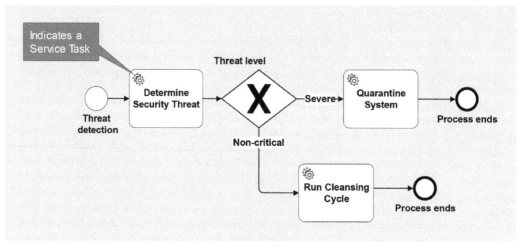

Figure 61: Applying Service Tasks—Cybersecurity Monitoring

Meditating Mike
Service Task Reflection

Take a moment before moving to the next exercise and ask yourself the following. Do I have a better understanding of service task? Does my organization automate any tasks? Are there redundant tasks I do today that could be automated? Would it be cost-effective?

Taking time to reflect on models you are analyzing will be an essential step as you begin making recommendations for process improvement, redesign, or re-engineering.

General Practitioner
Analyze and Decide Service Task Exercise

Let's examine our understanding of service task types and determine which service task types to apply to the following BPMN model.

In the following example, we provide a basic process model with no task types identified. We challenge you to rebuild the model and apply the service task based on your understanding of service tasks. Leave the task types blank if it is not a service task.

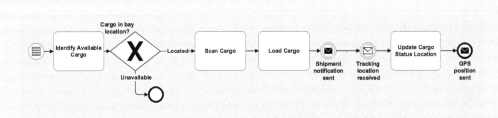

Figure 62: Identify the Service Tasks Exercise—Out Gate Cargo

- Rebuild the business process model with your identified service task.
  - Can you automate the complete process?
  - Do you think automation is always cost-effective?

Now that you have built the model and identified the service tasks, does it look like the following example?

We provide some of our insights into modeling with service tasks. Did anyone automate all of the tasks? Do you want to discuss automation further? Join our forum discussion regarding service tasks and automation.

The following is one possible solution for this exercise.

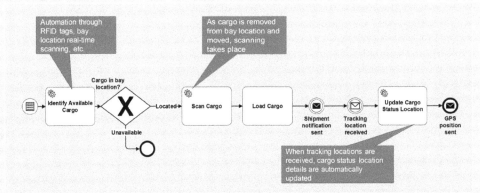

Figure 63: Solution for Identify the Service Tasks Exercise—Out Gate Cargo

With the progress being made in machine learning, artificial intelligence, and robotics, many of the tasks that we do today will be done by these technologies in the future. Understanding what the employee does versus automation is vital in capturing process details.

Surfer Dave Pro Tip

Bro, operations are great. How else do you think I get my daily forecasts on my weather application?

For those looking to expand their understanding of the task service, let's examine BPMN's service task *operation* from a web service perspective.

Web service operations, such as *GetWeatherForecastByLocation*, are important for Surfer Dave. This is because the operation lists which *messages are consumed.*

In this instance, the *GetWeatherForecastByLocationSoapIn* message updates the latest weather forecast for Surfer Dave at his current location.

It's important to note that operations can also *produce* messages. So, as you begin engineering a solution using BPMN, understanding what you can capture will be important for your model design.

3.1.3.4 Call Activities

We have discussed three task types thus far. In this section, we will expand our use of activities, by describing and applying the *call activity*. A call activity identifies a set of activities that have already been modeled which can be used in the process. We call these sets of activities a *global task*. We identify, or *call*, a global task when the activities should be executed. We will discuss the call activity for using a collapsed subprocess or (global process) in chapter 4. For now, we will focus on a global task being called to execute call activities.

The following are characteristics of call activities:

- Identified with a bold line around the activity shape (with or without a task type)

- Specifies the unique data requirements it must fulfill
    - For instance, we must provide specific *input* (data), and in return, we expect specific *output* (data) from the call activity

Figure 64: Call Activities—Three Types Depicted

If you are still learning BPMN, you are probably asking yourself, "Why and when would I use call activities?" Recall that these enable the reuse of activities that are completed within your organization and that can be shared globally.

Organizations have lines of business that have shared responsibilities. For instance, the shipping department identifies routes to move cargo and can estimate the transportation cost. A *call activity* allows modelers to represent that set of activities as a *reusable task*.

In the following example, we illustrate a basic process for selecting a course of action for the movement of cargo. We use the call activity *evaluate cost estimate* to represent a global task that is shared by other processes.

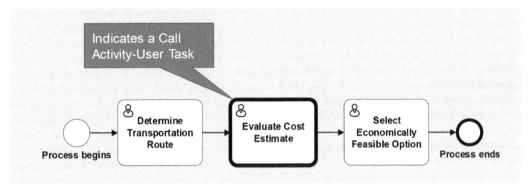

Figure 65: Application of User Call Activities

 **Streamer Seth** has created a video describing call activities. Join Seth as he builds and describes how to use the call activity.

Join us at https://www. tobpmpractitioners.com/videos. The videos match the figure name. You can also view our YouTube channel, *Joshua Fuehrer*.

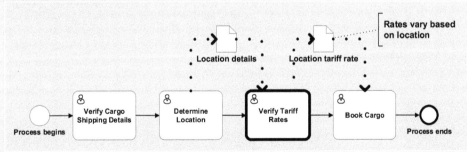

Figure 66: Call Activities Using BPMN

The key to identifying call activities is to think globally about that task. If a task is shared by other processes, it may be modeled as a global task (call activity). That global task can be invoked by other process models by using the call activity.

For those looking for a further explanation of call activities, we encourage you to join our forum discussion on call activities, or head to chapter 4. Both provide an expansion of this concept. In the next section, we dive into subprocesses and illustrate another layer of complexity with BPMN.

3.1.3.5 Subprocess Overview

If our goal were to create a process model of everything your organization does, we would not be able to create a diagram big enough to do it. It would be a colossal diagram that would wrap around the room and be impossible to follow. Luckily, we have subprocesses to expand or hide process details. In this section, we will describe collapsed subprocess, expanded subprocess, and how you can create a process model that might not wrap around the entire room.

A *task* is used when the work in the process cannot be broken down to a finer level of detail, whereas the collapsed *subprocess* (indicated with the plus) is used to illustrate that a process is decomposed into a lower level of details.

What that means is that there are two types of activities used in process modeling:

- Task (described in the previous sections)
- Subprocess

Subprocesses are used to represent an abstract of many activities or tasks in a process. As with task types, we only cover a small subset here to introduce you to the notation. In chapter 4, we expand on subprocesses as well. This section will cover two types of subprocesses:

- Expanded subprocess
- Collapsed subprocess

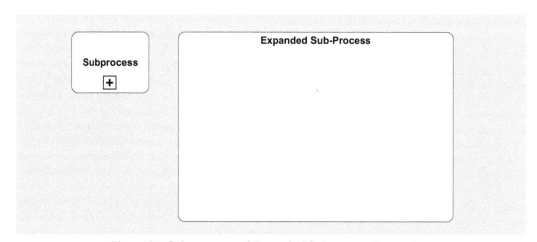

Figure 67: Subprocess and Expanded Subprocess Illustration

3.1.3.5.1 Collapsed Subprocess

We are in luck. Through the use of the *collapsed subprocess* notation, we can hide the flow details of our processes and capture a more strategic or tactical level picture of our organization's processes. The following are characteristics of a subprocess:

- Represented as an activity with a plus sign (+) in the lower center
- Only *none start events* can be used in subprocesses.
- Collapsed subprocess are used to hide the details of a process (sequence flow, activities, events, data, and gateways).

Subprocesses, as the name suggests, are a decomposition of a parent process. During our parent process flow, the parent process will trigger a subprocess when the sequence flow reaches the collapsed subprocess notation. We illustrate how the process flow goes from the parent process into the subprocess in the following example.

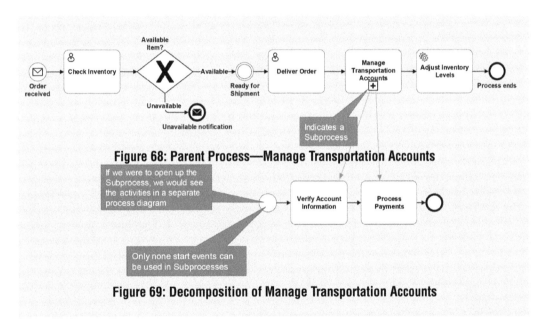

Figure 68: Parent Process—Manage Transportation Accounts

Figure 69: Decomposition of Manage Transportation Accounts

The subprocess helps reduce the complexity of BPMN. The examples thus far have been depicted as simple processes or the complex processes have been superficially modeled for simplicity. Modeling business processes typically results in complex models. Subprocesses reduce complexity by encapsulating details in separate models.

Have you ever tried to model your organization from the top down? If you think of your organization as a collection of subprocesses, you probably have.

At the highest level (think high-level workflow) you would see several subprocesses or main lines of business. In a transportation management business process model, it may look like this: Track Inventory Levels, Direct Cargo Operations, and Verify Transportation Accounts.

87

It is rare, however, that they fit neatly as in this first example:

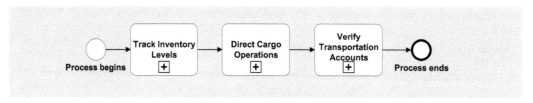

Figure 70: Simple View from the Top

The previous simple example could quickly look like the following model as you start peeling the layers of your organization and modeling out gateways and business rules.

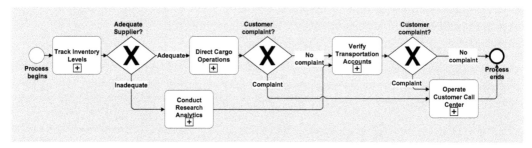

Figure 71: Expanding the View of Your Organization

You are probably asking yourself, "What good is modeling top-level processes? It just resembles our organization chart. What is the benefit?" Well, it does provide an enterprise view of your organization and, if done correctly, can identify redundant operations or organizational processes. Many of us in the field have been modeling processes at the lowest level. If that is the case, BPMN has you covered, and with a little analysis, you can reverse-engineer those business process models. Reverse engineering will enable you to quickly build enterprise-level models by rolling up activities into a model filled with collapsed subprocesses.

On occasion, you won't have all the information needed to completely model out a process. Using collapsed subprocesses allows you to capture the idea and come back later to fill in the details.

Surfer Dave Pro Tip

Understanding the parent and child relationship and using a centralized repository for storing primitives can greatly aid in your ability to determine a process hierarchy and reusing your enterprise assets.

How do you determine which activities fit neatly within a collapsed subprocess? Let's take a moment and practice identifying activities for a collapsed subprocess.

General Practitioner
Identifying Subprocesses in a Previously Built Process Model

Let's practice identifying tasks that could be grouped into a collapsed subprocess.

In the following example, we describe the process for writing a technical report—a standard process for consultants in the IT industry. Which tasks would logically go into a collapsed subprocess?

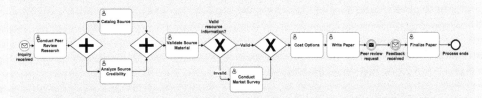

Figure 72: Identify the Collapsed Subprocess Exercise—Write a Technical Paper

We describe two practical solutions for creating collapsed subprocesses. Did you identify any others? If you did, join us on the forum discussion on subprocesses and share.

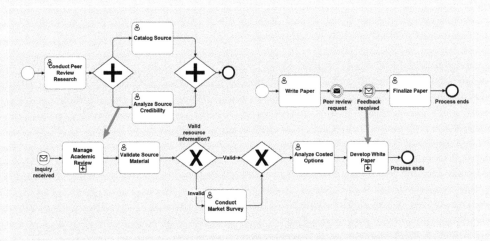

Figure 73: Possible Solution for Collapsed Subprocess Exercise—Write a Technical Paper

Using subprocesses can reduce the size of your model. Creating the collapsed subprocess may make sense for modeling, but there may be times when your functional community wants to see detail within the process model and not go to other models. In the next section, we describe the use of expanded subprocesses and how to apply them to those situations in which it makes sense to show the details of the subprocess.

3.1.3.5.2 Expanded Subprocess

We are commonly asked, "How do we model with the *expanded subprocess*, and should we?"

We have an interesting approach for applying the expanded subprocess. We think there is a benefit of showing details that represent the functional community and their activities. Expanded subprocesses add a lot of details, however, and make the model more complex. They also expand the work area or canvas size. As many of you may have experienced, expanding your canvas size usually equates to a more complex model. Combining a complex looking model with a poorly trained functional community is a recipe for a confusing, hard-to-follow model. Worse yet is the hand-wave when they say, "Yeah, this looks good," but in fact, it is not good, as they don't want to provide the validation required to ensure we have an accurate model. Without a precise model, there is little chance for a successful process improvement initiative.

The expanded subprocess enables task viewing within the main process flow. The following are characteristics of the expanded subprocess:

- Identified with a large, rounded rectangle

- Can use a start and stop event *(If you use an end event, you must also use a start event.)*

- Can have *floating activities*

- Sequence flows cannot come from the main process and cross into the expanded subprocess *(must stop at the edge of the expanded subprocess)*

In the following example, we depict our preferred way to model the expanded subprocess. We use the *start and stop* events to illustrate how the process begins and ends within the expanded subprocess.

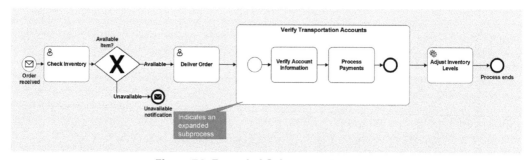

Figure 74: Expanded Subprocess Example

BPMN allows for an alternative way to model expanded subprocesses by allowing start and end events to be placed on the border of the expanded subprocess. The following is an example of the same model but using this alternative approach.

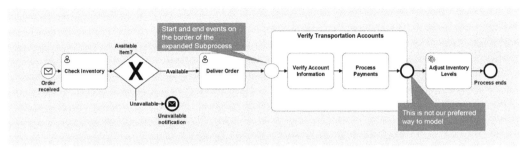

Figure 75: Expanded Subprocess with Start and End Events on Border

We want to advise that we avoid using this construct because it usually adds to the confusion, particularly when there is an inconsistency in its use. Therefore, we use start and stop events *within* the expanded subprocess, not on the border.

A question that surfaces on a regular basis is, "What if the activities in the subprocess are done in parallel?"

The expanded subprocess can be depicted with activities done in parallel. We use *managing sources* to illustrate how to use an expanded subprocess.

In the following example, we depict three activities that are done in parallel. Doing so has the same meaning as a *parallel gateway* (described previously), meaning that all three tasks are completed before the process flow continues out of the expanded subprocess and goes back to the parent-level process. The following depicts how you can model with the expanded subprocess with parallel tasks. An important note: start and stop events and sequence flows are optional.

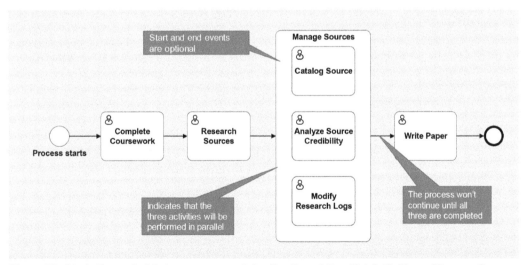

Figure 76: Study Expanded Subprocesses and Application of Parallel Activities—Manage Sources

Surfer Dave Pro Tip

Bro, in some instances, it makes sense to display the contents of a subprocess. The key as modelers is to determine when to display expanded subprocess details versus leaving it as a collapsed subprocess.

If you are still unsure, a few rules of thumb, we typically observe when modeling outside of a BPMN tool:

1. If you are using Visio, it is sometimes beneficial to show the details in the expanded subprocess to avoid the paper shuffle of going through multiple models.

2. If you have five activities or fewer, you can use a subprocess. The more activities, the harder the subprocess will be to display.

3. If using the expanded subprocess adds clarity for readers, then use it.

General Practitioner
When to Use an Expanded Subprocess Exercise

In my experience, one of the most essential things is to just do it. Model it. Because everyone makes mistakes at first and you need to go through this process, not just building, but analyzing your understanding.

The purpose of this exercise is to examine the records management business process model and apply the knowledge you gained in this section on expanded subprocesses.

- First, let's analyze which activities could be in an expanded subprocess:
  - Identify which expanded subprocess is done in parallel.

- Second, rebuild the following model using expanded subprocesses:

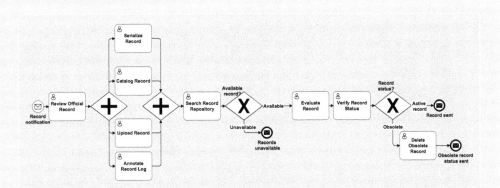

Figure 77: Identifying Use for Expanded Subprocess Exercise—Records Management

In the following example, we depict a possible solution for using expanded subprocesses.

We decided that the activities *serialize record*, *catalog record*, *upload record*, and *annotate record log* could be children of a higher-level or parent activity *manage official records*. We also decided that *evaluate record* and *verify record status* could be children of a parent activity *determine record status*. We came to that conclusion based on the nature of the activities. Had we been using a primitive repository, we may have seen that there was a parent-child relationship between these activities. Since we had to do this manually for the book, we made a judgment call based on our understanding of the BPMN rules.

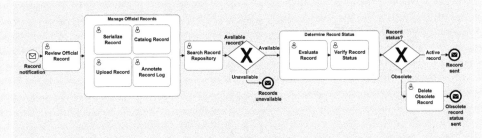

Figure 78: Possible Solution for Identifying Expanded Subprocess Exercise—Records Management

Meditating Mike
Reflecting on Subprocesses

Let's reflect on our actions. Take a moment and think about your process for identifying possible uses for the expanded subprocess.

1. Did you use the expanded subprocess correctly?

2. Did you identify that it may be better to use collapsed subprocesses?

3. Lastly, try to surface gaps in your knowledge. As you think about this, really ask yourself, "What doesn't make sense or what am I not quite sure about?" Jot those down. If you would like, share your comments on our forum page.

By identifying those gaps and sharing, we can analyze better ways to make meaningful connections and fill in those gaps by revising our training material and adding follow-up discussion on our website.

Sometimes using the collapsed subprocess is better for modeling. It will be case by case. Ask yourself, is it worth showing the information? Or can it be hidden? Modeling tools that allow quick access to the subprocess details will aid greatly in your decision. If you have a tool that exposes them, we would advise you to almost always hide the details, as it makes for a cleaner model. The following is how we would depict the previous example if we were using a modeling tool.

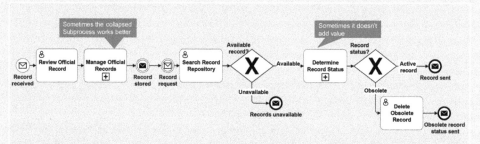

Figure 79: Reflect and Study the Use of Collapsed Subprocesses—Records Management

Studying Sara Activity

If you want to test your recall ability, I have created a self-assessment related to activities and tasks.

If you would like to challenge your understanding of activities and tasks, we have created a multiple-choice exercise that will test your basic recall ability for activities and tasks. Head to the training section on the website, and download the activity and task multi-choice test.

Surfer Dave Pro Tip

Bro, don't be fooled by the simplicity of this chapter or a big wave may knock you off your modeling board.

An important note to cover is that there are other types of subprocesses, such as *event subprocesses, transaction subprocesses*, and *call activity subprocesses*. We will discuss these in greater detail in chapter 4.

3.1.4 Swimlanes

We have focused primarily on modeling a basic business process with BPMN. In this section, we expand the use of pools and *swimlanes*. Specifically, we will describe the *pool* and the *participant*, and how these relate to process control. We then provide modeling opportunities to illustrate how we can start creating more complex business process models.

In BPMN, a pool represents a participant in collaboration.

- Participants can be a company.

- Participants used during collaboration can be partner roles.

  - Participants are responsible for the execution of a process, meaning they control when it starts, when it ends, and define the boundary of the process.

- Pools can depict a process (with process details) or can be depicted as a *black box* (no details).

In BPMN, a pool acts as a *container for a process* (sequence flows between events and activities). As a best practice, the process should have a name and be associated with the pool. A pool also represents a *participant in collaboration*. The participant should also be named and associated with an individual pool.

- Participants represent business-to-business collaborators and can be a company (partner entity) or a role in the company (partner roles).

- Participants can be nested in a pool using lanes.

- Participants are responsible for the *execution of a process*, meaning they control when it starts, when it ends, and define the boundary of the process.

- *White box pools* depict participants and the sequence flows and activity (process details).

- *Black box pools* depict a participant (business-to-business collaborator), but the details of the process are hidden.

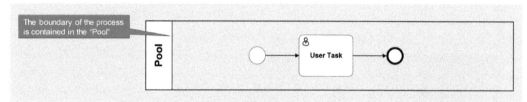

Figure 80: Pool with Process Details

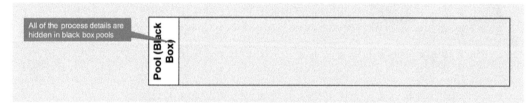

Figure 81: Black Box Pool—No Process Details

BPMN allows for the resizing of pools. An alternative way to depict a black box pool is by resizing it. When doing so, we are *black-boxing* the process, showing no details. You are probably wondering, "Why resize the black box pool?" There are many reasons, but the most obvious for us is that it reduces the size of the model canvas for process models showing collaboration.

Figure 82: Black Box Pool Resized

If you aren't using a tool that links data and processes, we have a way for you to add value to your resized black box pool. By using MS Visio, we are able to link the data from our database or Excel file to display value-added details for the customer regarding touch points. In the following example, we identify the participant and individual. As you begin connecting message flows to your black box pools, adding these details provides key touchpoint information.

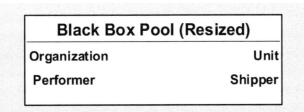

Figure 83: Expanding the Black Box Details for Resized Pools

Pools and *lanes* are used to organize the activities in a process. Lanes help identify roles, systems, and departments. Within pools, lanes help identify who is performing which specific activities.

- Lanes can represent:
    - Roles (supervisor, accountant, forklift driver)
    - Systems
    - Organizations, teams, or departments

- Lanes can be used to identify an organization, department, team, or role, whereas sublanes are usually used to identify the role.

A caveat to this: Whom you identify in lanes or sublanes will depend on the level of abstraction you are modeling (10,000-foot view versus 10-foot view)

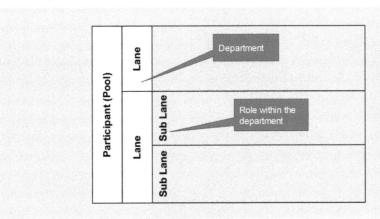

Figure 84: Pool, Lane, Sublane

At this point, we are introducing a new term, *orchestration model*, to describe the process (sequence flow and activity). Orchestration models specify how a single participant coordinates a set of activities.

Are there any sports fans reading this book? An uncomplicated way to view an orchestration model is with a football analogy. In the following example, the quarterback *calls* the play, the running back *runs* the ball to score the touchdown, and the kicker *kicks* the extra point. (Of course, as a football fan, the process described is a happy-day process, in which everything goes according to plan.)

Process orchestration is illustrated as follows:
- The pool assumes *process control* (the offense).
  - In the pool, the *offense* arranges for the process to begin (when a play is received).
  - The pool *offense* assigns the roles to the players.
  - The pool *offense* starts and stops the process.
  - Sequence flows cannot cross the boundary of the pool.

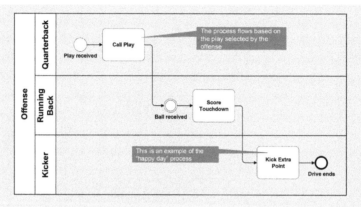

Figure 85: Process Orchestration—Football Analogy

General Practitioner
Building with Pools and Lanes Exercise

I learn more deeply when I actually model something that was project-oriented and everyone had a stake in making it work.

Let's practice building pools and lanes modeling out a generic accounting process. Your objective is to create a business process model for an upcoming project describing process orchestration.
- The *pool (accounting branch)* assumes control. The accounting branch controls three roles. Use three lanes to depict the following roles.
  - Invoice processor
  - Accountant
  - Supervisor
- The process begins with an *invoice received message* (event) by the invoice processor.
- The invoice processor *verifies the invoice* (task).
  - If the invoice is valid, the process flow moves to the accountant.
  - If the invoice is invalid, the process continues with the *invoice processor*, who *annotates the discrepancy* (task). The process then ends (event).

- – Use an *exclusive gateway* to depict the data-driven decision.
- The accountant *processes invoices* (task) that are valid.
- After an invoice is processed, the supervisor *confirms invoice accuracy* (task) as a mechanism to ensure compliance. The confirmed invoice is then used by the invoice processor to file the invoice (task).
- The process ends after an *invoice is filed* (event).

The application of pool and lanes was the main focus of this building exercise. While we used various cases during these early exercises, as many of you already know, extracting information from source documents or interview notes is not so simple. We try to incorporate various techniques to help you identify tasks, events, and gateways, as this is a crucial step when building out business process models from source documents.

The following represents a possible modeling solution. The importance of this exercise is the application of process orchestration and applying pool and lane concepts to your process model. Did anyone have a different solution? You will come to find our subjective nature will inevitably lead each of us to create models that are different than the next person.

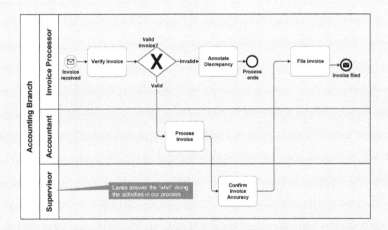

Figure 86: Create Accounting Branch Process Modeling through Process Orchestration Exercise

Before we continue, let's take a moment and explain BPMN's use of processes. BPMN has identified three types of business processes for orchestration: *private non-executable, private executable business processes*, and *public processes*. As we continue throughout this book, we discuss how to create internal (private) business processes and public processes for collaboration.

Private internal business processes refer to internal actions of an organization. The previous example of creating an accounting branch process model is an example of an internal business process (non-executable). An *executable internal business process* would have the activity mappings to, well, execute the model.

Non-executable just means we don't have enough details to execute the process in accordance with the semantics of BPMN (for example, expressions, described in chapter 4).

Public business processes refer to the interactions between two or more specific activities being accomplished by separate participants. The key to public processes is that the activities depicted on the internal model are limited to those used to communicate with the external participant. This means that we only depict activities that relate to message flows for public business processes. Internal business processes will have a greater level of details then public processes.

Surfer Dave Pro Tip

Bro, all these tourists are taking up my waves and crossing my boundaries.

These tourists are lucky that there aren't rules in place for crossing boundaries into my waves.

This reminds me of something similar you want to avoid with BPMN. Crossing lane boundaries with activities and expanded subprocesses is a violation.

The following example is an illustration of Surfer Dave's Pro Tip. When modeling process orchestration and using activities or expanded_subprocesses, we want to *avoid* crossing the boundary of the lanes and pools, as this is a violation.

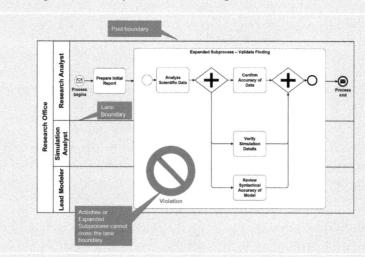

Figure 87: Surfer Dave Pro Tip—Expanded Subprocess and Lane Violation

Meditating Mike
Reflect on Your Organizational Connections

Take a moment. Let's reflect on your organization and the processes you are a part of. Read the following questions out loud and reflect on your responses.

Can you surface any of your own insights into a process in which there is more than one role (individual) contributing to the process? Do communication and interaction play a critical role in your process success?

What we find as we begin building business process models is that BPMN enables us to convey the knowledge of our workforce as they go about completing tasks related to a process. It is from that knowledge of those processes that organizations can gain a competitive advantage. Specifically, leadership can make key decisions that affect how processes achieve or maintain a competitive advantage by shifting resources, expanding on new capabilities, or leveraging organizational knowledge.

In the next section, we dive into some of the connecting objects you can use for your business process models.

3.1.5 Connecting Objects

In this section, we will describe the notation basic subset for *connecting objects*. We will start out by describing how to use *unconditional sequence flows*. Specifically, we will build on your previous knowledge of sequence flow rules. We will also expand on your current understanding of message flows and association, and illustrate how to effectively apply these to your process models.

3.1.5.1 Sequence Flows

If you have made it this far in the book, you should be familiar with *unconditional sequence flows*. "Why should I be familiar," you ask? Because you have already been applying unconditional sequence flows to your process models. While we cover conditional and default sequence flows in chapter 4, the basic rules discussed here apply to all three types of sequence flows.

Let's cover some basic sequence flow rules.

- Sequence flows describe the order of flow *elements* (tasks, events, and gateways) in a process.

- Pools, lanes, data objects, groups, and text annotations *cannot* have sequence flows.

The following example depicts basic sequence flow rules for tasks, events, and gateways.

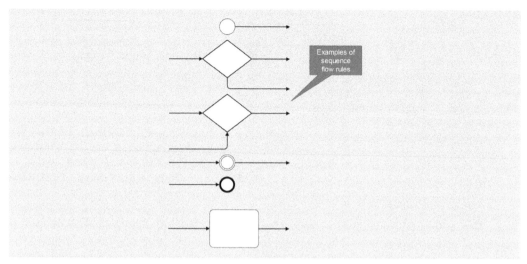

Figure 88: Typical Sequence Flow Rules—Preferred Modeling Style for Events, Activities, and Gateways

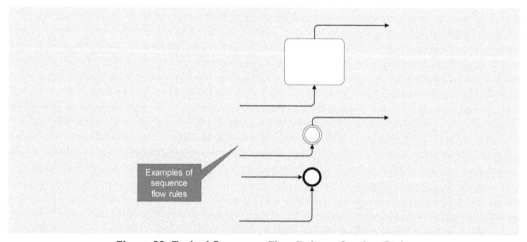

Figure 89: Typical Sequence Flow Rules—Another Style

Thus far, we have provided basic modeling techniques for sequence flows. The two previous examples depict the various ways sequence flows can be used. We typically choose to depict sequence flows from left to right, as our functional community finds them easier to follow. In the following section, we will expand on the use of message flows and how to use them for displaying collaboration between processes.

3.1.5.2 Message Flows

As business process modelers, we have a few notations in the toolkit that enable us to connect information within and outside of the process.

The first important concept for connecting information is the *message flow*. They are used to connect two or more processes. Message flows are also important because they help identify collaboration between two or more pools. The following is an example of the message flow connecting information from a black box pool.

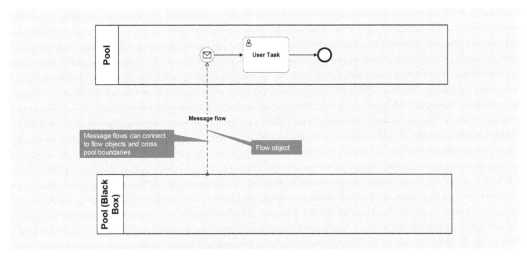

Figure 90: Message Flow and Collaboration

It is important to understand the rules of message flows between processes. The following are key message flow rules.

- Message flows *must* cross pool boundaries.
- Pools, catching events, throwing events, tasks, and expanded subprocesses can be modeled with message flows.
- Lanes, gateways, data objects, groups, and text annotations *cannot* have message flows.
- BPMN version 2.02 also allows for the *message* (envelope) to be optionally used on the message flow when depicting collaboration.

Message flows are the key to illustrating and communicating collaboration of processes.

You are probably saying, "But I only care about my processes." Ask yourself the following: Why does my process exist? Does it operate alone? Does my process rely on any resources or provide a service to someone?

The list could go on and on, but your process is a part of a greater good within the organization. Remember visualizing "the node"? Your processes are connected to other processes within your organization and connected to external customers, partners, etc. By using message flows, we can illustrate collaboration and the flow of information between processes, both private and public.

Streamer Seth has created a video describing *message flow rules*. Join Seth as he builds the following collaboration diagram highlighting the message flow connection rules.

Join us at https://www.bpmpractitioners.com/videos. The videos match the figure name. You can also view our YouTube channel, *Joshua Fuehrer*.

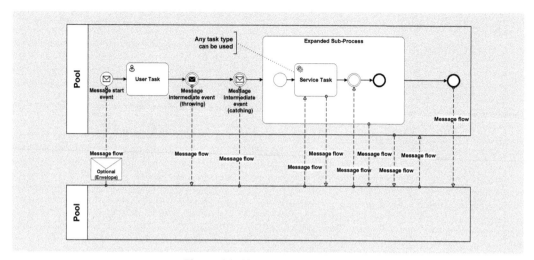

Figure 91: Message Flow Rules

As we discussed in the previous section, the collapsed pool is an alternative way to depict collaboration and black box communication. In the following model, we represent the message flow rules using the collapsed pool. As you will see, the same rules apply whether you are using the pool or collapsed pool.

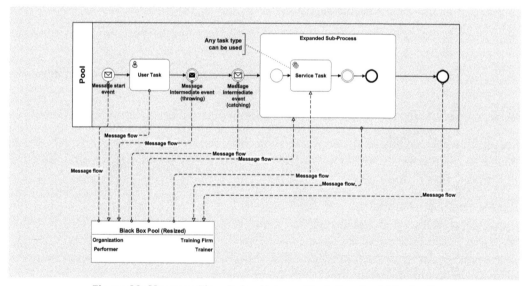

Figure 92: Message Flow Rules Using a Black Box Pool (Resized)

3.1.5.3 Association

We have already discussed *sequence flows* and *message flows*; the remaining notation for this section is *association*. Associations are used to connect information and artifacts, such as text annotations and data objects. We discuss text annotations and data objects in greater detail in the next section. Associations:

- Are used to connect information and artifacts with flow objects

- Can have no directional arrow, a one-way arrow, or a dual arrow

- Are used to show the input or output of data objects

Associations can also be used to show compensation from an activity (see chapter 4).

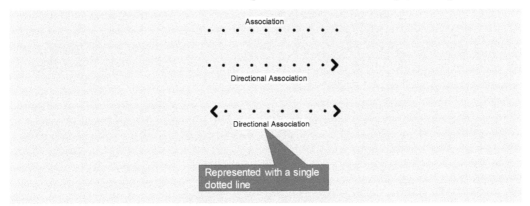

Figure 93: Association Example

In business, individuals are completing various tasks. During the completion of a task, a transformation occurs. The output from that individual activity or task results in the creation of something. BPMN enables us to depict what is being created from that hard work. For this section and the section on *data objects*, we will focus on a specific HR process to show the application of *associations* with data objects. In the following example, we depict a simple HR process in which employee paperwork is being verified.

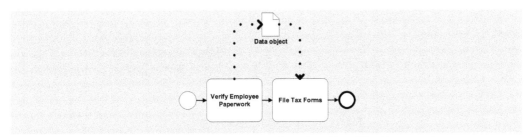

Figure 94: Data Object Example—Complete New Hire Paperwork

BPMN also allows for data objects to be associated with the *sequence flow connector*. The following is another example of how to connect to sequence flows.

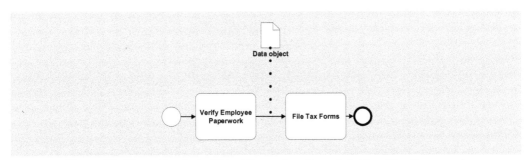

Figure 95: Alternative Data Object Example—Complete New Hire Paperwork

The output from the *transformation* of the activity is *data*, which can be physical or information. *Data associations* are used to show inputs or outputs of data objects. Associations are also useful for displaying data inputs or information required when beginning an activity.

Data associations are also used for data flows in or out of a data store object. The following example illustrates how data associations are used for depicting the flow of information to a *data store object*. In the next section, we will discuss the importance of data stores. It is important to understand that associations are used to ensure that data is retrieved or updated by the activities of a process.

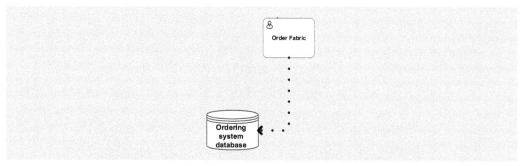

Figure 96: Data Associations and Connecting Data Stores

Associations are also useful for connecting artifacts. In the following example, we depict how associations are used to connect text annotations. *Text annotations* enable modelers to provide additional information for readers. Text annotations are covered in the next section in greater detail.

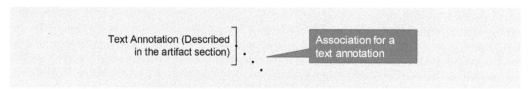

Figure 97: Text Annotation Example

While we don't dive into *compensation* in this section (refer to chapter 4), it is important to know that *associations* are key for connecting *compensation intermediate events* to *activities*. The following example provides a depiction of associations from compensation events.

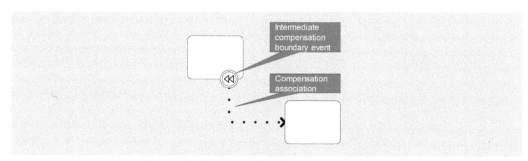

Figure 98: Compensation Association Example

The purpose of this section was to provide a high-level overview of associations and how you can use associations when creating business process models. In the following section, we will apply associations with their commonly used notation, *data*. There you will get to create process models combining both notations.

3.1.6 Data

In this section, we focus on the use of data in BPMN. There are two types discussed in this section, *data objects* and *data stores*. Data objects are the main notation for modeling data within your process or subprocess, whereas, data stores are a mechanism to add or retrieve information independent of your process.

We must add a caveat: Up until this point, we have slowly been building up the basic concepts of BPMN. In this section, we provide you an opportunity to dive deeper into the underlying meaning of data. We hope that by slowly incorporating some of the underlying elements and attributes throughout this book, we have enabled you to use that knowledge to create syntactically correct business process models and, if you so desire, dive even deeper through your journey of learning BPMN.

3.1.6.1 Data Objects

Data is important in BPMN. Data is the key to analyzing problems, benchmarking processes, and envisioning a *to-be* state for your organization's lines of business. The first data notation we will discuss is the use of *data objects*, which are used for modeling data within the boundary of your process. The following are four data objects.

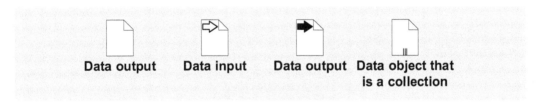

Figure 99: Data Objects

In the previous section, we used a simple HR process to discuss the data association notation. In the following example, we expand upon the data association and data object. We do this by labeling the data object *W2*, showing the transformation from one activity to the next. The process depicts at the completion of the activity *Verify Employee Paperwork,* a W2 data object is created from the activity, and that information is used to complete the next activity in the process, *File Tax Forms.*

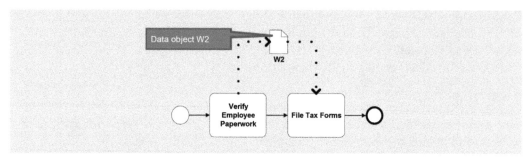

Figure 100: Data Object—Activity Transformation—W2

If only modeling were that simple, right? Luckily, BPMN has accounted for the complexity of data with the data collection object. Unless you are running a small operation, your HR department is typically busy. Orientation for new hires commonly occurs, in which an HR representative is probably handling many new employees. The following example depicts how to use the data object as a collection of many W2s. You will notice we used a notation we have not covered yet in the book: the *standard looping activity* notation. The standard looping activity represents that the activity continues to occur until all employee paperwork has been verified; each time it is completed, it generates a W2. To illustrate how a collection of W2s can occur, we felt it was appropriate to apply the standard looping activity. (We will dive deeper into the execution of the looping activity later in chapter 4.)

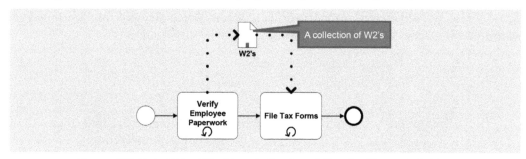

Figure 101: Data Object That Is a Collection of Standard Loop Activities

As discussed in the *data association* section, BPMN allows for a visual shortcut for connecting associations and data. In the following example, we complete our HR process using the *data association* connected to the *sequence flow*.

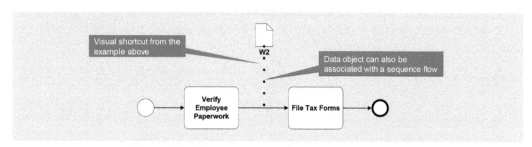

Figure 102: Alternative Data Object Example—W2

Data objects can be created, manipulated, and used during your process. The changed data is used to describe the different states of the same data object at different points in the process.

For example, the data object *W2* can be *reused* in the same diagram. As activities are being executed during the process, the *state* of the data changes. BPMN recommends using [square brackets] for referencing when a data object state changes. In the following examples, we first use *W2 [Submitted]* to represent that the state of the data changed for the W2 that was *filed* with the Internal Revenue Service (IRS). In the second example, we illustrate that the *W2 [Submitted]* is a data object output.

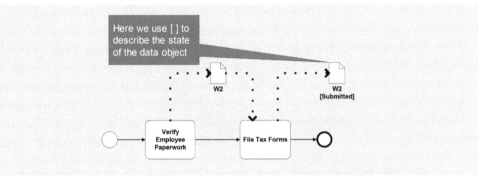

Figure 103: Data Object State Change—Adding Clarity to Your Process Model

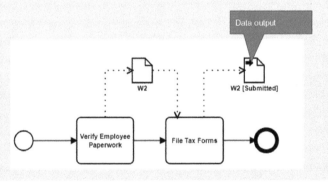

Figure 104: Data Object State Change and Data Object Output with Trisotech Modeler

Surfer Dave Pro Tip

Surf's up, Bro! I am ready to dive into these killer waves, but first, let's look at the item definition for a data object. Before you keep reading my gnarly insights, keep in mind, we are diving deep into the underlying characteristics of a data object.

All BPMN objects have underlying characteristics, and if Surfer Dave tried to explain each one, he would miss all the sweet waves. *Some* BPMN practitioners don't need to dive into these concepts yet. However, if you are ready to advance your understanding, then let's begin.

A notation that has an item definition element means there is a list of attributes that specify the structure of the notation.

So, if we break down the item definition for a data object, we will see that there are three attributes:

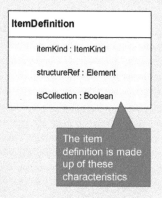

Figure 105: Surfer Dave Pro Tip—Class Object for Item Definition for Data Object

Let's start with understanding *ItemKind*. In the following example, we illustrate the two types of ItemKind for the data object. We have physical and information, represented by the nature of the item.

Physical = papers, paperwork, W2, or application.

Information = data, email, or digital ID.

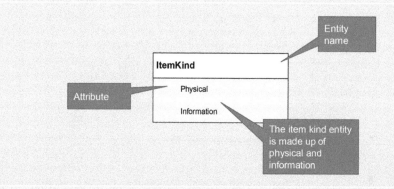

Figure 106: Surfer Dave Pro Tip—ItemKind Explained for Data Object

The second attribute is *structureRef*, which is stating that this element is a data object.

The third attribute is the collection which is set by a *Boolean*, which means that there are two possible values. Boolean values are usually defined as either *true* or *false*. So, if our data object *is* a multiple collection, it would be set to *true*.

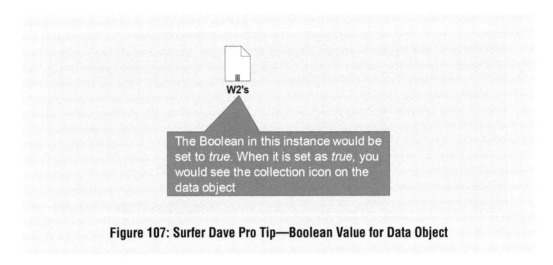

Figure 107: Surfer Dave Pro Tip—Boolean Value for Data Object

In the following section, we expand our understanding of data by examining the data stores, and how to model with the notations covered in these sections.

3.1.6.2 Data Store

Data Stores are used by activities to *create*, *read*, *update*, or *delete* (CRUD) data. The activities can retrieve information from data stores that can be warehouse databases, supply chain systems, passenger reservation systems, and so on.

Figure 108: Data Store

To get a better sense of why data stores are essential, we depict a process using the data store in the following example. In the ordering process, we identify three performers completing a set of activities. We illustrate how inventory lists are checked and how an associate buyer orders fabric. Since the order system's database lives outside of the process, we used the *data store* to indicate that order information is being updated in the database. Alternatively, we also depict how information is retrieved by the manager when validating purchase orders.

Could the associate buyer just hand a purchase order to the manager? Sure, but in today's complex business processes, having systems in place to automate the simple, mundane task improves the productivity of processes. It's when those organizations improve the efficiencies of their processes that competitive advantage can be seen and studied.

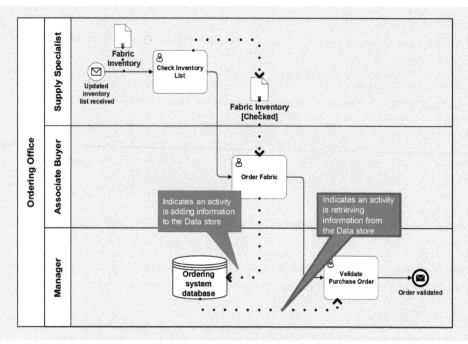

Figure 109: Examine a Business Supporting Process—Manage Textiles

General Practitioner
Experience Using Operating Procedures to Create a Process Model with the Data Notations

You have two options: You can read the latest DHS regulation, which is about 400 pages, or use the following operating procedure to create a process model using data objects.

If you are like us, you will probably choose the latter. As business process modelers, we are tasked with going into organizations, examining business process, and developing process models. Sometimes, processes are documented through operating instructions or through a nonsanctioned operating procedure created by who knows whom?

In the following exercise, use your knowledge of data to create a BPMN model.

Summary: You have been tasked with modeling out the current process for the Passport Processing Office. The department head stated that staff members are so busy they can't take time to be interviewed but have an operating procedure for you to use to model out their process. Use your knowledge of data objects, events, and any other notations applicable to model out the following steps.

Steps Outlined in the Operating Procedure
Diagram the **Passport Processing Office**.

- The process starts when the passport specialist receives a passport application.
  - A passport application consists of an individual's details (*see checklist 149994*).

- Once an application is received, the passport specialist shall *evaluate* passport application.
- Once the application is evaluated, the passport specialist will decide if the application is *valid* or if there is missing information.
  - If there is missing information, the passport specialist will email the applicant regarding the missing information, and the process ends (*all resubmissions start over*).
  - If the passport application is valid, the passport specialist *submits* a [verified] passport application to the passport processor.
- Once a [verified] passport application is received by the passport processor, the passport processor will *approve* the passport application. Approved applications are *updated* in the DHS's *passport database.*
- The process ends after the *end of the month* and after approved passport applications are *documented* in a *manual spreadsheet* kept on the passport processor's computer (*which occurs the first day of the next month*).

So, we have to be honest, an operating procedure is almost never this simple. Most are full of jargon or redundant information; even worse, they can be several pages long. The purpose here was to illustrate how you could take a page out of a procedure to identify concepts you could use for modeling with data. The following is a potential solution based on our understanding of the operating procedures.

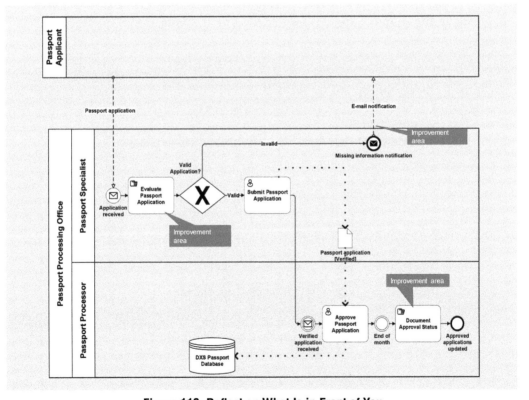

Figure 110: Reflect on What Is in Front of You

Meditating Mike
Using Reflection to Solve Problems

Take a moment and really look at the model. Take a few deep breaths and ask yourself did you see anywhere that you would improve on this process?

As a business analyst creating business process models, it is important that you examine the processes you are modeling. Identifying areas for improvement and discussing potential choke points in the process will enable experts in the field to have their own *aha* moment for a deeper conversation when creating that future vision of their organizational process.

3.1.7 Artifacts

This section describes the unique application of *artifacts* with BPMN. We describe the nature of the group icon and expand your understanding of text annotations. Artifacts are used to convey additional details about the process. BPMN identifies the *text annotation* and *group icon*.

However, BPMN also enables modelers to use other artifacts. This is because artifacts have no *syntax value* when modeled. The key to using artifacts is that they add additional details or clarity for outside readers. We have seen a variety of artifacts over the years. We will conclude this section by discussing some of our favorites uses for the group icon and text annotation.

Figure 111: Text Annotation with an Attached Association

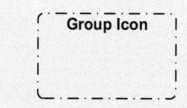

Figure 112: Group Icon Illustration

Text annotations enable models to provide more details. "What details?" you are probably asking. If any details add value to your customer, then add them. We have found a variety of uses for text annotations. We identify two uses in the following example.

In the first, we identify that cargo is received in location bay 55. Why would we do this, you ask? From a process improvement perspective, identifying areas of potential choke points or problem areas enables smarter decisions to be made. In the second, we identify that hand receipts are signed via tablets. If we are having problems with the receipt of cargo for a process, identifying additional details allows for an examination of that activity. For instance, is it a problem with the tablets (system-specific) or is a lack of training and material the culprit? Documenting that tacit knowledge, along with other important information, can aid in effectively analyzing organizational processes.

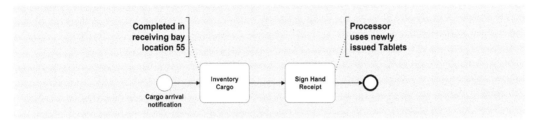

Figure 113: Uses for Text Annotations—In-Check Cargo Example

The *group icon* allows for the grouping of various objects on the model. This is particularly useful when grouping together activities, decision points, and events, as well as articulating additional details for reviewers. Additionally, the group icon is beneficial because it can cross pool and lane boundaries. This means as modelers, you can group together information important for studying process collaboration. In the following example, we describe how training activities occur in our online collaboration lab.

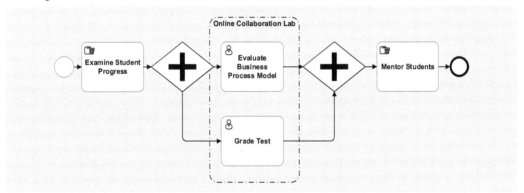

Figure 114: Application for Group Icon—Develop BPMN Student

Meditating Mike
Reflecting on the Application of Artifacts to Improve Your Process Models

Take a moment away from reading and take five deep, slow breaths. Take this moment to really think about your previous modeling experience and ask yourself the following.

Is there any other way I would use these artifact concepts to further enhance the models I create?

The following are a few uses for group and text annotations.

- Application of text annotations
  - Completion time for activities
  - Identification of pain points in the process
  - Identification of metrics significant to the process (costs, resources, etc.)
  - Clarification of process activities
  - Identification of opportunities for improvement
- Application of group icons
  - Identification of locations where activities are completed
  - Clarifying steps in a process

Join **Streamer Seth** as he describes a few ways you can use artifacts to improve your business process models.

Join us at www.bpmpractitioners.com/videos. The videos match the figure name. You can also view our YouTube channel, *Joshua Fuehrer*.

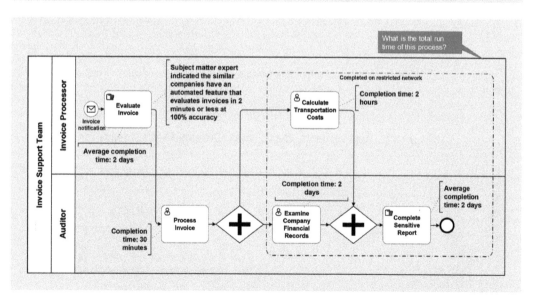

Figure 115: Run Time for the Transportation Invoice Process

Let's imagine trying to calculate the process runtime by capturing metrics with the assistance of text annotations: Use the previous example and calculate run time.

Given the current days and hours provided, does anyone know how long the run time of the current process is?

Answer: Six days and thirty minutes. The reason is the parallel process will not be completed earlier than two days' time. So, 2 + 2 + 2 + ½.

Before we move on, let's examine one more custom artifact and how you can use it for your modeling efforts. We discussed the pool dilemma earlier. By using a custom artifact and Visio, we can identify the processes we are depicting for our organization. We use *folder* (or *package for you* Unified Modeling Language experts) to depict our process name.

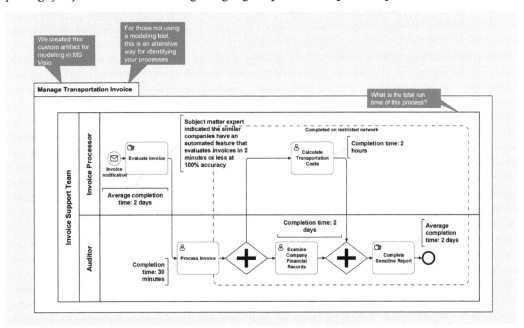

Figure 116: Custom Artifact for Depicting the Organization Process without a Modeling Tool

Meditating Mike
Reflecting on Poor Modeling Practices

After you have reviewed the video (Run Time for the Transportation Invoice Process) *and the previous model, take a moment and reflect. Close your eyes and take a few deep breaths. Ask yourself what the impact would be if improper notations were used in the process.*

When incorrect notations are used, it can cause errors in model validation and simulation. Errors in modeling result in the consumption of resources needed to fix and revalidate business process models. Additionally, as we build out business process models, members will have various levels of understanding of BPMN, so using improper notations will instill bad modeling habits for those using your models as baselines throughout your organization.

It is important to note that unless new practitioners have modeling skills and a deep understanding of BPMN, they may fall into the trap of learning from previously built business process models. A well-built model can be tremendous in transferring the explicit knowledge of an organizational process and proper modeling techniques.

By the same token, a poorly built model can transfer those same bad habits to a new practitioner. How many times have you used a previously developed model as a baseline or seen a concept modeled, assumed it was right, and copied the technique? We can tell you from personal experience, at one time or another, *we* have. Let's hear from you. Join our discussion on the forums regarding the impacts of modeling errors. What have you experienced?

Studying Sara
Pools, Lanes, and Message Flow Multi-Choice Exercise

I have created a multi-choice test as it relates to pools, lanes, and message flows that will help identify correct use of all three of these concepts.

Now that you have seen the importance of pools, lanes, and message flows, let's test that knowledge with a multi-choice exercise. We have created an exercise to test your ability to conceptualize correctly modeled processes.

Join us at: https://www.bpmpractitioners.com/bpmn-exercises

3.1.8 Team Collaboration and Learning BPMN

Learning BPMN can be challenging for anyone. We have to admit, early on, we saw members within our organization struggle with the interpretation of the BPMN specification and from the various material available online describing different concepts. However, that struggle taught us a valuable lesson: through collaboration, we could discuss our interpretation by creating a model together. We would then use that model as a team to examine the underlining meaning in which we could challenge or validate one another's views, usually with the BPMN specification.

Consultation Team Exercise Introduction

Let's demonstrate your ability to *analyze* proper use of BPMN through the following consultation exercise. Imagine your team has been tasked with reviewing an already-developed business process model. For this exercise, as a team, evaluate the following model for BPMN:

- Identify discrepancies
- Identify potential areas for improvement
- Recreate the model with recommended improvements

Please head to our website to download a more readable copy from our training material section. Download consultation service request 1:

https://www.bpmpractitioners.com/bpmn-exercises

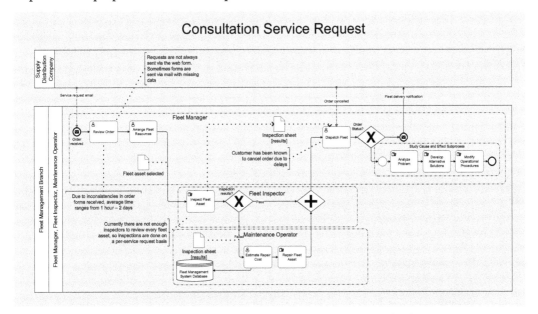

Figure 117: Consultation Service Request—An Exercise in BPMN Collaboration

The second thing you need to do is find a **group**.

There are several ways to do this. If you are process modeling in an organization, seek out colleagues using or learning BPMN, or go to our forums page and post that you are looking to collaborate on this experience.

Once you have your *group* (at least three people), share this exercise with them. After you have had time to review the model, share your recommendations with your group.

Within the training section, we provide a possible modeling solution but refrain from peeking until you have recreated the model and discussed your recommendations with your group.

The following solution highlights changes in *green*. Did anyone find anything else? If so, join us on the forums and share your solution. Additionally, before you share, ask yourself, what would you recommend to the process owner to improve this process?

For example, the organization could improve *lag time of the processing of orders* by creating a *web form* and *automate the process* to ensure missing information did not occur for the first activity (review order). Another improvement identified is that another process could be created to handle *fleet inspections* annually/quarterly to ensure demand is always met.

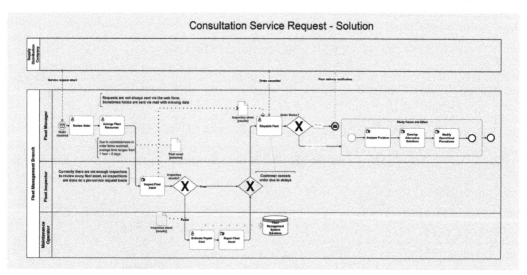

Figure 118: Solution for Consultation Service Request—An Exercise in BPMN Collaboration

Meditating Mike
Reflect on Different Views

After you have completed the consultation exercise as a team, take a moment to reflect and ask the following.

1. Did team members have any different views on the discrepancies identified?

2. How did you reconcile differences?

An essential concept for team learning and collaboration is the ability to communicate effectively. By sharing your views on why you think the notation is used a certain way or how to model a certain problem, you are exposing your level of understanding. Doing so in an open dialogue can promote a greater level of understanding as a team. That level of understanding can be used to improve the process models being developed and facilitate a culture of team learning. As we proceed through the remaining chapters, we will provide these types of collaborative experiences to promote a deeper level of understanding and promote team learning.

3.2 Closing Reflections

This chapter was an introduction to key notations used for business process modeling. We identified and applied a basic palette for you to use for business process modeling. The intent of this chapter was to instill basic modeling practices and establish the foundational knowledge structure of a small BPMN subset.

If we were successful, your transition through the next chapters will bring about a greater level of understanding and an evolution will occur as you move up the spiral of knowledge, building your understanding of BPMN.

Finally, as you take time to reflect on your experiences so far, we encourage you to evaluate your progress as it relates to the goals you set. This is particularly important before moving onto the next chapter.

If you want to assess your goals, join our goal-setting group on the forums and download the BPMN Personal Mastery Goal Scale:

https://www.bpmpractitioners.com/bpmn-forums-and-resources/goal-setting-1

There you can answer a few questions about where you are today and how you can shape future goals.

In the next chapter, we dive deeper into BPMN and what it has to offer through an examination of the practical application of BPMN and specific notations that will round out your modeling notation subset.

4. Expanding the Application of BPMN

4.1 Advanced Process Modeling with BPMN

Based on our experiences with modeling and evidence from the research community, we will devote this chapter to expanding your knowledge of key notations and concepts relevant to advanced business process modeling with BPMN.

What do we mean by "advanced"? To us, advanced implies a decomposition of our main lines of business into a level of detail that reveals the true complexity of the process. As we dive deeper into complex processes, we need the ability to model *exceptions* to the process flow, business rules, and so much more. The following includes some of the notations we will cover in this chapter.

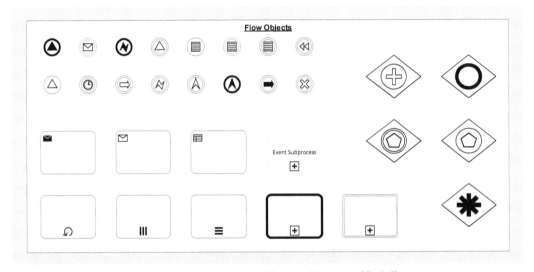

Figure 119: Notations for Advanced Process Modeling

All of you BPMN practitioners out there are probably asking, "Where are the compensation tasks, cancel end events, and ad hoc subprocesses?" Don't worry, we will cover these in this chapter. The challenge was how to get all of the notations in chapter 4 on one model because there are *a lot*.

Before we begin, let's establish another set of goals.

4.1.1 Tokens

Hopefully, you have made it through the book so far with no problem. If so, great, because we are about to dive into a BPMN concept that is theoretical and can only be visualized with good modeling tools or a great imagination. The BPMN concept we are referring to is the *token*.

The BPMN specification defines tokens as a theoretical concept that is used as an aid to define the behavior of a process that is being performed.

Through sequence flows, tokens are passed between activities, gateways, and events. As a process starts, a token is created. The token *traverses* the process through the sequence flow to activities, events, and gateways. At the end of the process (end event), the token is *consumed*. A token does not pass through a message flow.

In the first example, we describe how to visualize a token. We are fortunate that the tool we use, Trisotech modeler, allows us to do process animation to follow the token.

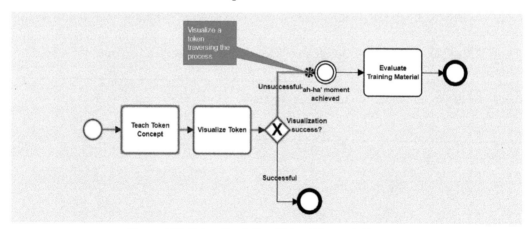

Figure 120: Token Depiction Using Trisotech Modeler

As we visualize the token, we begin to see how the token traverses the process.

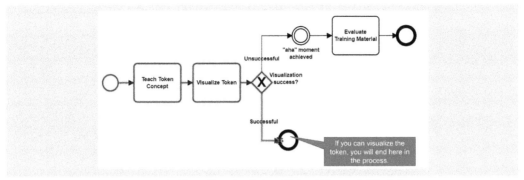

Figure 121: Visualize the Token Using Trisotech Modeler

Understanding tokens can be beneficial as you start modeling—specifically as process paths diverge and become complex. Visualizing the token can help mitigate process deadlocks. In the following example, we depict a token after two passes through a parallel gateway. When a token arrives at the parallel gateway, two tokens emerge and traverse one path each.

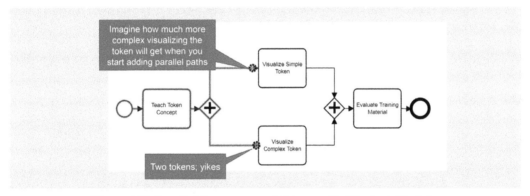

Figure 122: Parallel Processes and Tokens with Trisotech Modeler

This application is where *visualizing tokens* is helpful. In this instance, the second token remains at the activity until it is completed. Remember, for parallel gateways, all active paths must *synchronize* before the process can continue down the path. In the following examples, we depict how the first token remains at the *parallel join*, waiting for the remaining active token.

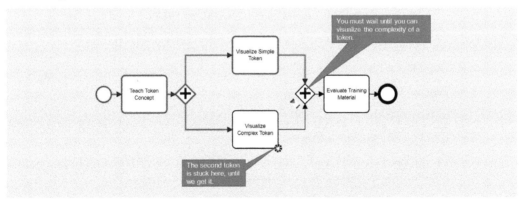

Figure 123: Token Merge with Trisotech Modeler

Hopefully, tools within your organization allow you to visualize tokens. They are particularly useful when examining redundancies, deadlocks, or business process modeling logic in your BPMN models. If you don't have a snazzy tool, we hope this discussion provides some insight on how you can visualize the token.

4.1.2 Events

Up until now, we have covered some of the most commonly used event types. In this section, we will expand on your understanding through the practical application of the remaining event types. For the sake of simplicity, we have broken out events into two sections.

In the first, we cover events that occur during a normal process flow. After that, we dive deeper into the application of *boundary events* and introduce the concept interrupting and noninterrupting events.

4.1.2.1 Conditional Events

Processes are filled with conditions that occur based on changes to states, both internally and externally. *Conditional events* are used to illustrate these state changes. As conditions become true, they can trigger the start or influence the flow of the process.

Does anyone invest in the stock market? The following is a simple example of how to use conditional events.

We tell our broker to sell if the stock decreases by 40 percent. In our model, we set a condition: when true, our stock is sold. We use the *intermediate conditional event* to illustrate that we want no further transactions made until *sale confirmation* has occurred. Once that condition is true, our process continues, and we begin to evaluate stock options.

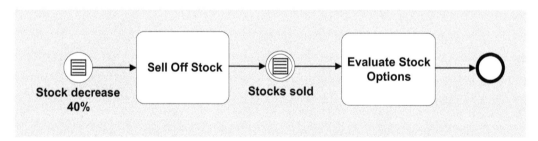

Figure 124: Illustration of Conditional Events

The following are characteristics of conditional start and intermediate events:

- Depicted as lined paper
- Triggered when the condition becomes *true*
- Can be used to start an in-event subprocess
- Can be used to start a top-level process
- Conditional events can be start events, intermediate catching events, interrupting events, and noninterrupting conditional events (cannot be end events).

General Practitioner
Building with Conditional Events

For me, the most important learning experience is learning by doing.

Learning by doing is very important, but make time to reflect on that action.

Let's use *conditional events* and build out the following invoicing business process model. For this exercise, just recreate the invoice model.

Here is our scenario. After the cargo is booked for shipment, we have to check the invoice. If we find discrepancies, they have to be resolved before we submit the invoice. But there is an additional condition—that the shipment must be complete before we can submit the invoice. Here is our logic. To start the process, we use a *conditional start event,* because when the condition *cargo booking* is set to *true,* and the event occurs, the process begins.

The first step is to *validate billing charges.* We model two paths using an exclusive gateway (we either have a discrepancy, or we don't). If there are discrepancies, we *update invoice details.* We use a matching exclusive gateway to merge our process flows. We use a *conditional intermediate event* to illustrate that we must wait on the condition *shipment arrival* before our process continues. So, until the condition occurs, the *token* waits at that event. Once the condition is true, the process continues, and we can submit our invoice.

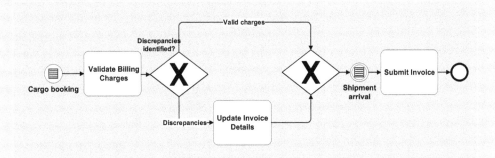

Figure 125: Recreate Invoice Model with Conditional Events

We think conditional events are instrumental and can be used to model many everyday situations. In fact, like many other practitioners, we use conditional events and incorporate these into our subset of commonly used modeling notations.

We don't spend too much time on conditional events in this section, as we include conditional events in many of the practical application exercises in the following sections.

4.1.2.2 Link Events

Linked events are useful when modeling complex processes and are used to connect two segments of a process. Link events allow modelers to connect the sequence flows without actually using a sequence flow. In the following example, we depict what we mean.

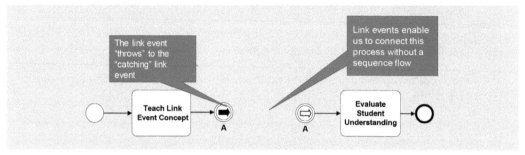

Figure 126: Explaining the Concept of Link Events

The following are the characteristics of the link event:

- Only occur in the normal process flow
- Used to avoid long sequence lines
- Can only be used for same process level linking
- Use *throw and catch* concept (using black and white arrows)
- Great for looping process flows (*annotate a looping flow for clarity*)

A common question we hear is, "Why should we use link events?" Typically, we use link events on larger process models in which a gateway or boundary event diverges the process, and the steps of that process flow do not occur until later. In that instance, we use the link event to avoid long lines across our model.

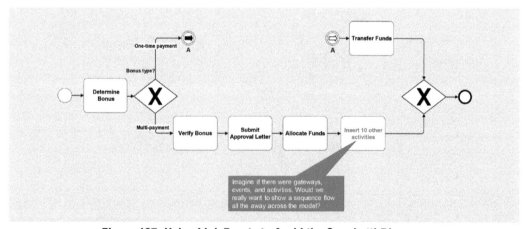

Figure 127: Using Link Events to Avoid the Spaghetti Diagram

Another great use for the link event is the looping of processes. To illustrate this below, we use a generic simulation process for analyzing strategic plans for a company. We identify the analyst and simulation specialist with various tasks they complete in parallel. When the analyst requires simulation, we use the *link throw event A* to link to the simulation specialist with the *link catch event A*. When the simulation specialist completes *model simulation*, we use the *link throw event B* to link back to the analyst, depicted with the *link catch event B* using the link event, reducing the sequence flows crisscrossing.

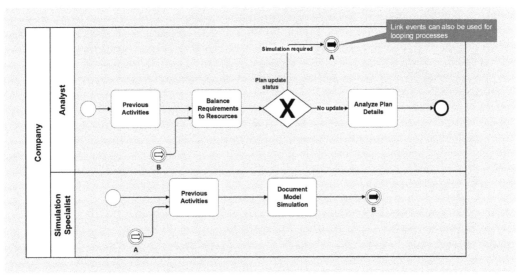

Figure 128: Application of Looping Process Flows with Link Events—Strategic Planning Example

General Practitioner
Thinking Outside the Box

Regarding enforcement, the most relevant thing is the practical application of the notations we learn.

Let's use link events to recreate a business process model.

Do you have any old BPMN models that are large?

If so, attempt to update that model with *link events*. Once you have updated the link event, have a colleague look at the model and solicit feedback. Specifically, ask your colleague, "Does this update help the readability or look cleaner?" If you don't have a colleague, join us for the link event forum discussion. There we can collaborate on your model.

If you don't have a previous model, that's OK. Use the model from the team collaboration exercise in chapter 3.

Meditating Mike
Analyzing Previous Models

Think about how you analyzed what you could link to the previous exercise. As you were reviewing your previous model, did you see anything else you would improve?

Reflecting on previous experience or in this case, previously built models, enables us to take a fresh approach to updating and refining your models. The key is to make time to analyze your models.

4.1.2.3 Signal Events

Signal events are used to model messages that have no specific target. When using a signal event, there is no specific person that the message is directed toward. Instead, it can be viewed as a message to the masses—similar to social media notifications.

Here is our scenario. An employee updates an inventory system, and the system sends out an update notice. One way to model this scenario is by using a *signal event*. The employee sends the signal as a *general notification*. Any users of the systems will see the signal as an updated system notification.

The signal event has several characteristics:

- Does not require a source: may or may not be from a participant
  - Signals can be system notifications, general alerts, flare guns, distress beacons, smoke signals, etc.
- Displayed with a diamond
- Can be start events, intermediate throw-and-catch events, boundary events, noninterrupting boundary events, and end events
- Can be used to start an event subprocess
- Can be used to start a top-level process
- Can carry data
- Can start multiple processes

Have you used any social media platform? We have. These are great for communicating, but also can be very daunting. Luckily, the *signal event* seems to have been made for social media. When someone shares something on the internet, unless privacy controls are employed, it usually is open for anyone to see.

In the following example, we illustrate how the *signal start event* works. The *social media notification* is made available, and if we see it, it starts our process. At the end of our process, if we decide to share the social media post, we make it available to the world with no specific target audience.

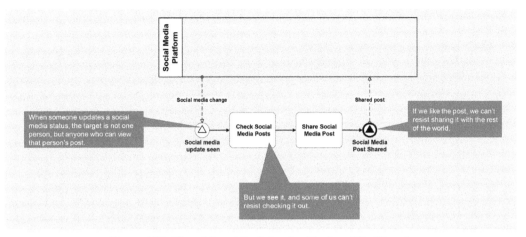

Figure 129: Signal Event Explained—Start and End Events

Meditating Mike
Previous Experience with Signal Events

Let's examine previous experiences from this book. Take a moment and try to recall where else have you seen signal events in the book.

Were you able to think about the early example of signal events described by Surfer Dave in chapter 3? We defined two different processes in which signal events could be used. While we did not dive into the specifics then, we will now take a moment and illustrate why signal events were used for those examples.

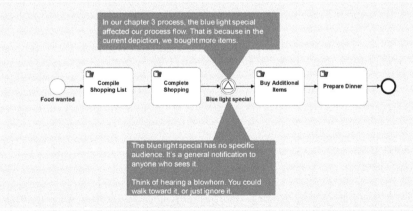

Figure 130: Previous Experience with Signal Events—Blue Light Special

The second example was our chores process. Here we illustrated that the washing machine completion alert affects how our process continues. We used the signal event because the washing machine alert is just a general notification. We are sure in the future some of those smart washers will send text or app notifications.

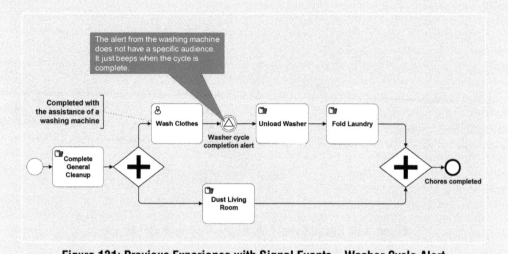

Figure 131: Previous Experience with Signal Events—Washer Cycle Alert

Forum Felicia
Shared Insights for Signal Events

There is a great question and answer in a forum post regarding signal events.

There is a great discussion on sending messages to multiple pools and the applicability for signal events. As you read the responses, take a moment and think about the nature of signal events and how you may apply it to the forum discussion:

https://groups.google.com/forum/#!topic/BPMNforum/6KSf7M0qntg

While we don't usually like to jump ahead, we do provide a good exercise in the *event-based gateway* section, in which you get to apply signal events. We held off on creating an application exercise here, primarily because we like to show the applicability of signal events in more complex process modeling exercises.

4.1.2.4 Multiple Events

In the next two sections, we will look at *multiple events* and *parallel multiple events*. We have to confess, in our years of process modeling, we have yet to find a home for these notations in our subset of regularly used notations. We will explain why from our BPMN practitioner lens after we discuss some basic characteristics.

The *multiple events* have several characteristics:

- Displayed with a pentagon
- Have multiple event definitions, meaning out of the multiple events listed, only *one* needs to be triggered

- Can be used to start an *event subprocess*
- Can be used to start a top-level process
- Can be start events, intermediate throw and catch events, boundary events, noninterrupting boundary events, and end events

We depict our first illustration of a multiple event in our planning process for high-impact projects. The process can start multiple ways, either from a new requirement, a rejected plan, or when a crisis is identified. Only one of the event definitions must be met to start this process. As the process continues, we can *throw* back to the participant, requesting additional details or a clearance request. Again, multiple events can trigger or occur and move our process along. Similarly, only one event needs to be "caught" to move onto the *prioritize resources* task. The process ends with one event definition throwing information to a participant.

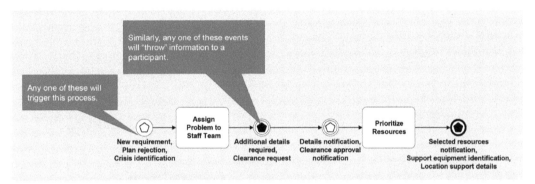

Figure 132: Multiple Event Depiction—Plan Project Example

General Practitioner
Multiple Event Practice Problem

Keeping it simple allows for successful modeling sessions with subject matter experts (SMEs) who are better able to understand the basic notations.

Let's apply the *multiple event* notation to the following problem. Your manager has just indicated that there is an issue with expense reports and wants you to model and analyze the problem. The manager provides you with the following information.

- The process can begin when:
  - An email is received stating there is an action item in the reporting system, *or*
  - A phone call is received indicating that a report has been uploaded
- *Task 1:* The first action requires the accounts manager to *review system information.*

- If no report is displayed, then the account manager must email system help desk

   > The account managers will receive a *troubleshoot detail email* **or** will receive a *report upload notification.*

      o Either message requires the accounts manager to *review system information* (Task 1 again).

- If a report is displayed, then the accounts manager (*Task 2*) *verifies report accuracy.*

- *Task 3*: The account managers will *certify report.*

- The process ends after the account manager completes certifying the report. The system generates a notification indicating a record has been certified.

Take a moment without looking ahead and try to model out these steps using multiple events.

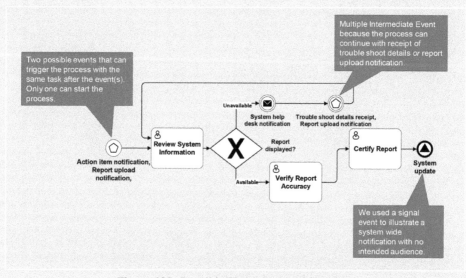

Figure 133: Possible Multiple Event Solution

How did your solution compare to ours? Hop on our forums and share your thoughts, specifically if you found another interesting way to model this problem using multiple events. Before we move onto parallel multiple events in the next section, let us share our thoughts on multiple events.

Here is what we struggle with as BPMN practitioners with multiple events and parallel multiple events. The following model shows the same process with other participants. There are a lot of message flows associated with the model, and that is why we struggle with multiple events and parallel multiple events. Unless you are dealing with only one participant, using multiple events, the model can get quite confusing to reviewers. Trying to show all of the participants can make the model very complex.

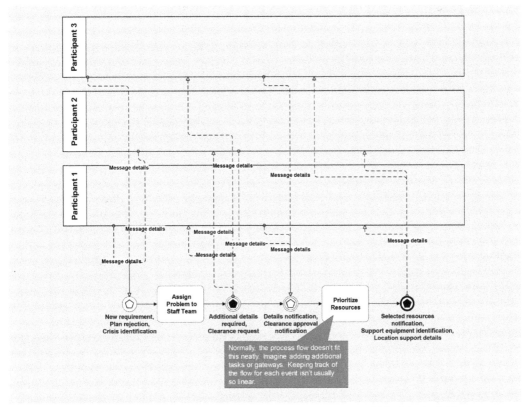

Figure 134: Evaluating the Application of Multiple Events—A Modeler's Critique

4.1.2.5 Parallel Multiple Events

Parallel multiple events share similar characteristics of the multiple event. Parallel multiple events are designed to have more than one event definition, meaning they can have several occurrences associated with the event. The key difference with parallel multiple events is that all of the events definitions associated must occur before the process flow can start or continue.

The parallel multiple event has several characteristics:

- Displayed with an outlined plus (these are only *catching events*), reminiscent of the solid plus of a *parallel gateway*
- Has *parallel multiple event definitions*, meaning all the events listed need to occur
- Can be used to start an event subprocess
- Can be used to start a top-level process
- Can be start events, intermediate catch events, boundary events, and noninterrupting boundary events

We have found that we use parallel multiple events even less than multiple events. The main reason is that to trigger the event, *all* of the events listed must occur. We find that situation in business to be rare, particularly in today's fast-paced environment.

To illustrate how to use parallel multiple events, we depict how our process begins with buying a new car. We see car ads on TV all the time, but it is not until we see a friend pull up in the same sports car and we hear him or her rave about it that our process to buy a car starts. Similarly, for intermediate parallel multiple events, it is not until our car and all of the car accessories are delivered that we will complete the customer survey.

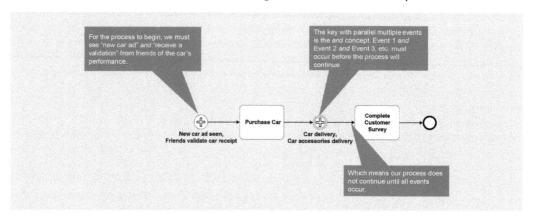

Figure 135: Parallel Multiple Event Illustration—Buying a Car

In the next section, we will expand on the use of events by describing *boundary events*.

4.1.3 Boundary Events and Expanding Your Application of Events

An important concept introduced in BPMN is the use of *boundary events*. There are two types of boundary events: interrupting and noninterrupting. In this section, we will discuss how to use boundary events while expanding your understanding of events by introducing a couple new event types that we have not discussed. We continue to peel away at another level of complexity within BPMN and share our experiences with some key concepts.

4.1.3.1 Interrupting Boundary Intermediate Events

Thus far, we have discussed the *normal process flow* of your business processes. Let's examine the happy-day path for booking and loading cargo.

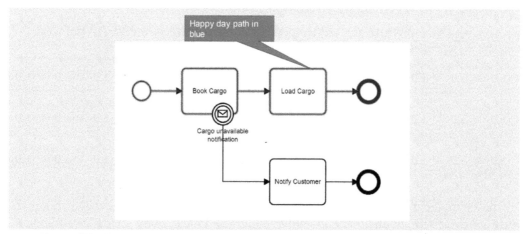

Figure 136: Happy-Day Path with Trisotech Modeler—Introduction to Boundary Events

What happens when the person you are interviewing says, "But sometimes when cargo is not available to load, we have to notify the customer." Aha: an exception to the process. The exception is the key premise for boundary events, as it enables the creation of *exception flows*.

The following are characteristics of boundary events and how to model boundary events:

- Attach an *intermediate event* to the boundary of an activity.

- Use intermediate boundary events when an exception in the process occurs.

- Boundary events change the *normal flow* into an *exception flow*.

- Place an *outbound sequence flow* from the event.

In the following example, we describe how to apply a boundary event and create an exception flow. When an exception is identified, we place the message intermediate event on the boundary of an activity. We place the sequence flow describing the exception flow, which leads to an alternate activity, *notify the customer*.

Now let's expand on boundary events by examining what happens when a boundary event is triggered. When *cargo unavailable notification* is triggered, a downstream token is generated, and the exception flow leads to the alternate step (in this case, *notify the customer*). The previous activity, *book cargo*, is canceled (never finishes) based on the value of its *cancelActivity* attribute (see Surfer Dave's Pro Tip on Page 139 for more information on these attributes).

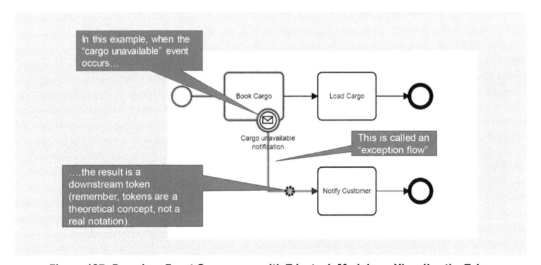

Figure 137: Boundary Event Occurrence with Trisotech Modeler—Visualize the Token

General Practitioner's Exception Flows

Let's practice using boundary events by recreating the following process model.

In this example, we just want you to practice placing the message intermediate event on the boundary of the activity to create an exception flow. .

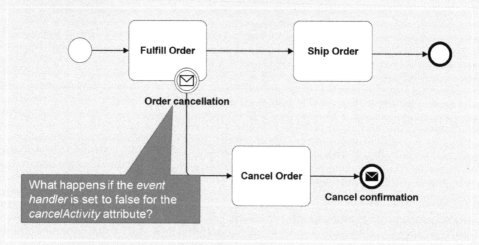

Figure 138: Apply Boundary Event Concept to a Cancelled Order

Surfer Dave Pro Tip

Bro, I have all of these exceptions for when I want to shred waves—like, when there is a rare shark sighting, it's an exception to my process which results in me waxing my boards.

Let's take a look at the details behind these exceptions. Here we dive into the attributes of the boundary event and the activity to which it is attached. This tip is for those who want to dive into the water and examine the complexity of the underlying BPMN syntax.

Let's start with the *intermediate event attached to the boundary of activity* from the previous cargo example. When the condition *cargo unavailable* is set to *true*, an exception to the process flow is triggered when the event occurs. Setting conditions are useful when modeling in tools capable of applying these rules. (If you are using Visio or tools that do not have this capability, then just describe the event as best as possible to describe when an exception is triggered.)

For the activity, if a message, signal, timer, or conditional event is attached to the boundary, the activity *may or may not be canceled*. It will depend on the *cancelActivity* attribute and if it is defined as a *true* value. This means that even though you have depicted an exception flow in your process, the normal, happy-day process path could continue if the boundary event is not triggered.

In the previous book cargo example, how could that be possible? Well, one example is that the shipment arrives and is booked. In that instance, all the cargo arrived, and no exception occurs.

For the remainder of the boundary event section, we will assume that all event handlers are set to true, so, any interrupting boundary events will cancel the activity, and we will examine the exception flow.

4.1.3.2 Noninterrupting Events

Noninterrupting events are unique in that they do not disturb the normal process flow. Noninterrupting events can be used to start event subprocesses or be placed on the boundary of an activity. The key point is that they do not interrupt the process; rather, a *new token is created* in which additional steps are completed. We will cover the basics for the noninterrupting events, but the main focus of this section will be to illustrate how to use the *boundary noninterrupting event*. We describe the noninterrupting start events in greater detail in the event subprocess section later in this chapter.

As the name implies, noninterrupting events do not interrupt the activity. Rather, when the *cancelActivity* attribute is set to *false*, a new token is generated when the event occurs, and we see a new process path.

The following model describes how to use noninterrupting boundary events for our manufacturing process. As we begin to manufacture a product, we receive a new inventory item. In this instance, we use the noninterrupting message event attached to the boundary of the activity. A new token is generated when the message event occurs, and we see that a new sequence flow leads to another activity. The main happy-day path still continues, but because we received that message, we have an additional step in our process.

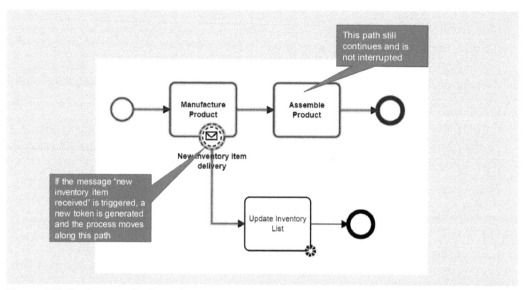

Figure 139: Noninterrupting Boundary Events with Trisotech Modeler—Basic Manufacturing Process

If you grasp and understand the interrupting boundary event, modeling with noninterrupting boundary events is a piece of cake. Noninterrupting boundary events:

- Attach a noninterrupting intermediate event to the boundary of an activity
- Use noninterrupting intermediate boundary events when the cancel activity is set to false
- Create a new token and sequence flow path from the boundary event
- Place outbound sequence flow(s) from the event
- Noninterrupting events are depicted with dashed lines
- Can be used to start an event-subprocess
- Can be used within the normal process flow

Surfer Dave Pro Tip

Bro, I need to take a break after that last killer wipeout. I guess it's a good time to discuss noninterrupting boundary events.

When the event occurs, the associated task to which the event is attached continues to be active. There are different ways to handle this situation. First, the flow is merged back into the main flow of the process which is shown in Figure 140. However, we prefer to end the noninterrupting boundary event path with its own end event, if we know it does not merge back into the happy-day path, which is shown in Figure 141.

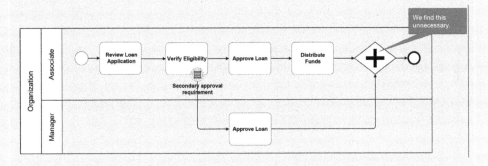

Figure 140: Merging a Noninterrupting Boundary Event Process Path—Loan Process

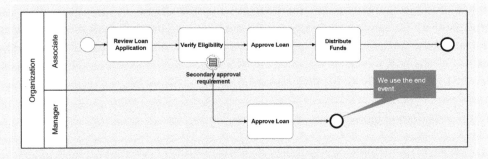

Figure 141: Preferred Way to Model Noninterrupting Boundary Event Process Path— Loan Process

Meditating Mike
Thinking About How You Build Process Models

After you have reviewed our two ways to model with noninterrupting boundary events and how to merge them, close your eyes and take a few slow deep breaths. Clear your mind.

After your mind is clear, reflect on the following.

1. Now that you have seen two ways to handle the sequence flow and process path for noninterrupting boundary events, do you have a preference for how you would model?

2. Do you have an alternative way you would model?

Thinking about rules and guides for process modeling will help improve your organization's process for modeling. Take, for example, organizations that have a *style guide, modeling rules* and *guidelines* and a disciplined approach to modeling. These simple things, when thought out and applied consistently, will reduce the syntactical errors in your organization's modeling efforts.

4.1.3.3 Application of Boundary Events

While the previous section described an overview of boundary events, we saved the in-depth application for this section, mainly because in this section we introduce several new notations that you can use for boundary events. In this section we will introduce you to the *error, escalation, cancel,* and *compensation* events and demonstrate how you can apply these notations to your business process models. But first, let's examine how we can apply boundary events to some of the previous events from chapter 3.

4.1.3.3.1 Boundary Intermediate Timer Events

In this section, we examine how to model *intermediate timer events* placed on the boundary of an activity. When a timer is used in a normal flow, a *boundary event timer* retains the same timer event definition. The difference is that when the timer event is attached to the boundary of the activity, a new process path emerges when the timer event occurs. In the following illustration, we describe how, at 2:00 p.m. daily, if the activity *complete shipment documents* is not completed, a new token is generated, and an *exception flow* leads us to *identify problems.*

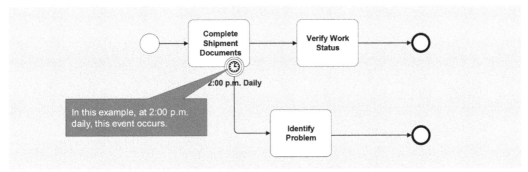

Figure 142: Applying Interrupting Boundary Events for Timers

Now let's expand on this concept a little bit further by describing how noninterrupting timer events work. Imagine the subject matter expert you are interviewing states, "Well, after two hours, while we are identifying the problem, we have to create an incident log record." Using the noninterrupting timer event enables us to create an additional path for the creation of an incident log while we continue to identify the problem.

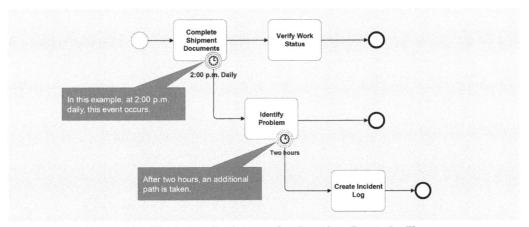

Figure 143: Illustrating Noninterrupting Boundary Events for Timers

Forum Felicia
Noninterrupting Timer Event Discussion

Are you feeling comfortable with timer events and applying them to the boundary of an activity? If so, there is a great discussion on timer events at the link listed.

We highly recommend you read the following forum post. If you want to contribute to the body of BPMN practitioner knowledge, we encourage you to respond if you can share your insight. Communicating with other BPMN practitioners is an effective way to expand upon your understanding and share your understanding with the BPMN community:

https://groups.google.com/forum/#!topic/bpmnforum/FoUGwPG1JNc

4.1.3.3.2 Boundary Intermediate Conditional Event

We often see the *conditional event* in our business process models. This observation aligns with the research community and their findings that out of models surveyed, conditional events are a very commonly used notation. Conditional events occur in a normal process flow; *boundary conditional events* occur when a *conditional event definition* occurs. To illustrate the *interrupting boundary conditional event*, we use the cargo loading process to show that while loading cargo, if the mission is canceled, a new token emerges that requires us to *inventory cargo*. The *mission canceled* occurrence generates a new *exception flow*. If the mission cancellation never occurs, our loading is complete, and we can transfer cargo ownership.

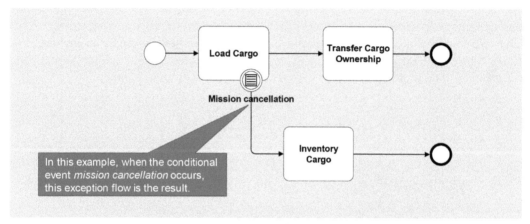

Figure 144: Applying Interrupting Boundary Events for Conditions

When we demonstrate the noninterrupting conditional boundary event, we see that as we inventory the cargo, we noticed a damaged item. A new token is generated and the cargo is identified and isolated (*frustrated*), along with the inventorying of any remaining cargo.

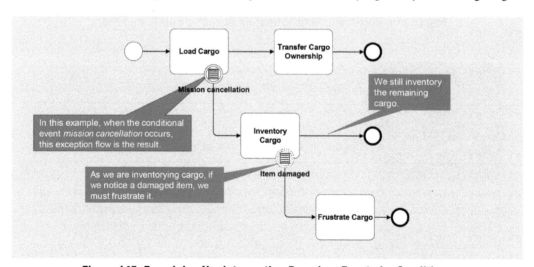

Figure 145: Examining Noninterrupting Boundary Events for Conditions

Forum Felicia
Collaborating on Interrupting Event Types

I need your insight! There is a forum post regarding interrupting event types. While the practitioner asks several questions, there is one interesting question regarding boundary conditional events.

We highly recommend you read the following forum post:

https://groups.google.com/forum/#!topic/bpmnforum/ro01DGdA6VM

We encourage you to respond if you can share your experience with modeling interrupting boundary events.

4.1.3.3.3 Boundary Intermediate Signal Event

We expand on the *signal event* in this section by picking up where we left off with our obsession with social media. The application of signal events placed on the boundary of activity enables the creation of an *exception flow* from general notifications received during the process.

As we discussed in the previous section, signal events can be used for general system notifications. There is no specific target, but a general notification is sent for anyone to see. In the following depiction, as we review our social media page, a new alert comes across to all users as a trending article. We illustrate that this new, shiny object or *news article* is an exception to our normal process, and we instead review the news article.

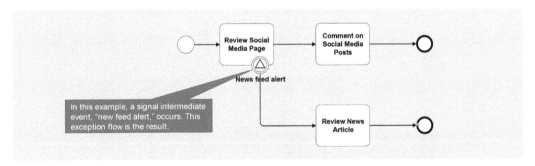

Figure 146: Applying Interrupting Boundary Events for Signals

Let's expand upon this model a little by introducing noninterrupting boundary events using the signal notation. As we review the news article, a *car ad alert* displays across the banner of the article. This time, to illustrate the noninterrupting boundary signal event, we create another process path in which we review the car ad and continue to review the news article. (We can multitask.)

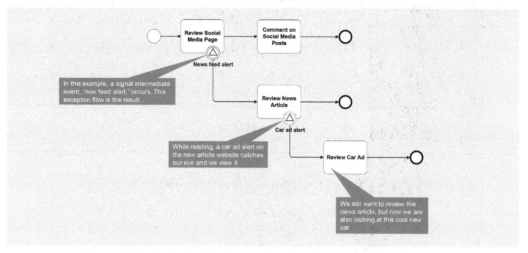

Figure 147: Analyzing Noninterrupting Boundary Events for Signals

Join **Streamer Seth** as he describes how to apply signal events. Follow along while he creates a model using the signal event. This will give us a moment to discuss in greater detail how to apply signal events to the boundary of an activity.

Join us at https://www.bpmpractitioners.com/videos. The videos match the figure names. You can also view our YouTube channel, *Joshua Fuehrer*.

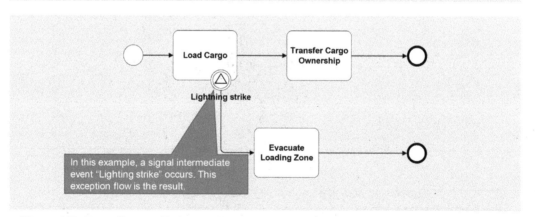

Figure 148: Expanding our Understanding of Boundary Events using Signals—Video Example

4.1.3.3.4 Compensation Events and the Compensation Task

Compensation events are unique with BPMN. We are able to illustrate the power of modeling by developing complex process models with compensation. In the next two sections, we will illustrate how you can use *compensation events* and *compensation tasks* for process modeling.

We will also provide some of our insightful experiences regarding these two notations.

The *compensation event* has several characteristics:

- Used to undo a previously completed task
- Can be used as an *interrupting boundary event* for exception flow
- Can be a start, end, or intermediate event
- *Throwing compensation events* refer to the process in which they are depicted. Basically, the *throw* event is encapsulated within the process and throws to the *catch boundary interrupting compensation event* (see the following model).
- Use associations (not sequence flows) to attach compensation events attached to the boundary of activity to connect compensation tasks.

The *compensation activity* has several characteristics:

- Can be a task or subprocess
- Shown with a two-triangle marker pointing to the left
- Undoes the previous task

Let's start with the basic concept of *compensation events* and how to model them. The following model illustrates the basics for *compensation events* and *compensation tasks*. The *boundary event compensation catch* is only triggered by a *throw* which comes later in the process. When the compensation event is triggered, we use an *association* to connect the compensation task, which then reverses the attached activity. In this case, it reverses the effects of the *process bonus* task—as if the activity transformation for *process bonus* did not occur.

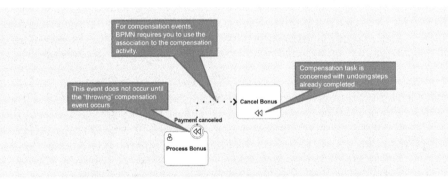

Figure 149: Understanding Compensation Events and Tasks

Since compensations can be daunting to newer BPMN practitioners, join **Streamer Seth** as he builds a business process model using compensation. Here, the yearly performance process is modeled out.

Join us at https://www.bpmpractitioners.com/videos.

The videos match the figure name. You can also view our YouTube channel, *Joshua Fuehrer.*

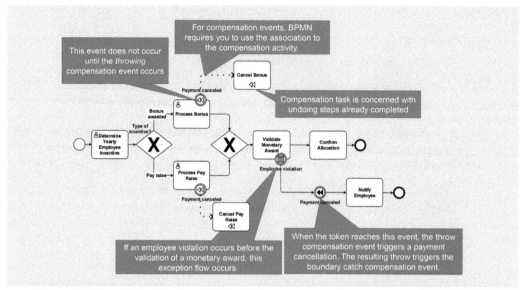

Figure 150: Examining the Complexity of Compensation—Yearly Performance Process

To illustrate all of these moving parts and the concept of compensation events and activities, we depict the yearly pay raise or bonus process for the human resources department. Typically, performance reports are used to determine employee incentives. In the example, we determine an employee can receive two possible incentives. As the process steps are completed, we ignore the *intermediate compensation boundary events* attached to the *process pay raise* and the *process bonus* user tasks. We do so because compensation events attached to the boundary are ignored until the throwing compensation event occurs (if ever).

It is when the task *validate monetary award* is being completed that if the condition *employee violation* occurs, an exception is triggered which leads to the compensation throwing event that triggers a payment cancellation. The resulting *throw* compensation event goes to the *catch boundary compensation event*. We use the association to connect to the boundary event and compensation task (in this instance, *cancel bonus* or *cancel pay raise*). The compensation task then reverses the previous activities' effect.

4.1.3.3.5 Error Events

In this section, we discuss error events and how you can model the *error event* for your business processes. From a practitioner standpoint, we have observed the error event can be misunderstood and misused. Before we dive into its subtlety, however, let's discuss some of the error event's characteristics. Intermediate error events:

- Can only be placed on the boundary of the activity
- Can be used to end subprocesses
- Always interrupt the activity
- Are used to signify a critical problem during the process of completing an activity
- Can be used to start an event subprocess

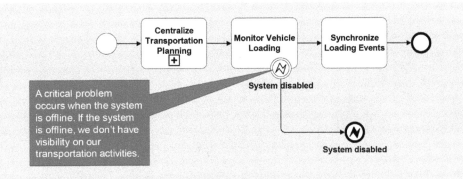

Figure 151: Examining Error Events for a Reverse Logistics Operation Center

General Practitioner
Application of Error Events Experience

Watch out! Errors will occur through overuse of the error notation.

Let's explore error events further by building out a phase of a scenario planning process. The following example depicts the project preparation stage of scenario planning.

On the boundary of the very first activity *define scenario scope*, we place the *error event* to identify a discrepancy between what we have and what is needed to complete the task. The reason why we use the error event is some critical piece of information is missing, and the task cannot be completed. Basically, we are signifying through the use of the error event that this is not a common occurrence, but a *critical problem* that can occur, particularly when stakeholders' requirements are lacking.

Now go ahead and practice applying an error event to the following example.

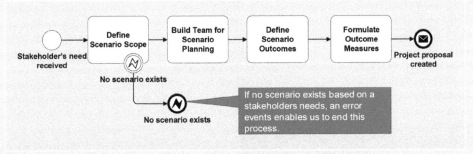

Figure 152: Application of Error Events for Scenario Planning Project Preparation

Surfer Dave Pro Tip

Whoa. The use of error events is unique in that error events can have an error code or no error code *assigned to the parent process.*

Remember that error codes really only apply if you are using a modeling tool that allows you to capture the *error, error code, item definition, item nature,* and *definition type.*

The importance of using error events correctly cannot be overstated. We have seen countless models cluttered with error events. It's not to say that all were right or wrong: it's that error events should be reserved for cases when there is a serious error in the process, not for any ordinary condition.

Are you looking to see how we apply error events to the boundary of expanded subprocesses? Join **Streamer Seth** as he demonstrates how to apply error events within an expanded subprocess.

Join us at https://www.bpmpractitioners.com/videos. The videos match the figure name. You can also view our YouTube channel, *Joshua Fuehrer.*

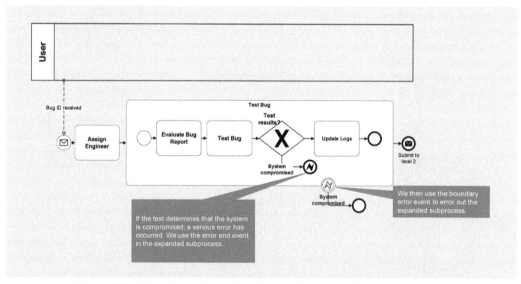

Figure 153: Using Error Events for System Bug Reporting—Video Example

Forum Felicia
Leveraging BPMN Templates and Expert Examples

There are so many different resources available to us BPMN practitioners. Did you know OMG has a BPMN forum page that lists process modeling templates?"

We are a huge fan of what OMG and its community members are doing. OMG has a great website full of templates provided by other BPMN practitioners. If you want to expand your understanding of how to use error events, the BPMN group under their templates section has an Amazon fulfillment process that does a great job illustrating error events in action:

https://www.businessprocessincubator.com/content/amazon-fulfillment/

4.1.3.3.6 Cancel Events

Cancel events are a unique notation as they are used in transaction subprocesses. Cancel events are used to end the transaction subprocess because an activity within the transaction subprocess could not be completed.

The cancel event has several characteristics:

- Can be intermediate boundary events on transaction subprocesses or end events within a transaction subprocess

- Interrupts the activity it's attached to; the cancelActivity is always *true*

- Can only be used for transaction subprocesses

- Can lead to compensation of the activities in the transaction subprocess (*see Transaction Subprocess section*)

Figure 154: Transaction Subprocess

We will dive deeper into *transaction subprocesses* later in this chapter.

For now, we will cover how the cancel event is applied to the following supply chain management process. The following example illustrates three activities that occur within our *conduct warehouse optimization* transaction subprocess. We use the *error event* (indicating a serious problem) with the activity *determine picking strategy*—in this case, that we don't have a picking strategy available. That error triggers a new process flow, which cancels the transaction subprocess. We didn't use compensation in this instance, as we did not need to roll back the actions taken. In the transaction subprocess section, we will dive into rolling back process activities.

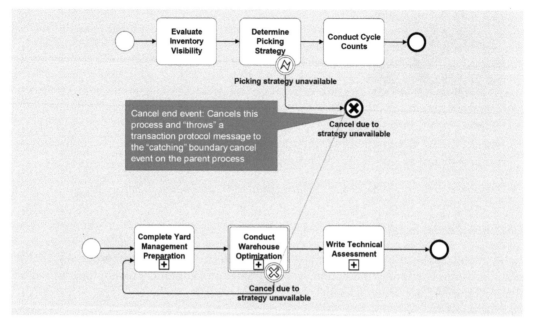

Figure 155: Application of Cancel Events on the Parent and Child Process—Supply Chain Management Optimization

The cancellation results in a *throw* to the parent process. We are then able to use an *intermediate boundary cancel event* to cancel the transaction subprocess and generate a sequence flow to the *complete yard management preparation* collapsed subprocess.

The yard management folks didn't have a strategy available for us to complete our process. Typically, the cross flow of information would occur in your organization, but even the smallest event that can have a huge impact is accounted for using cancel events. That is where the power for modeling with cancel events resides. We will get into the details of the transaction subprocess and why this allows us as modelers to capture the smallest event which could have the greatest impact on our process later in this chapter.

Forum Felicia
Group Discussion on Cancel Events

If you are looking to see how other BPMN practitioners interact regarding complex notations, join the following BPMN forum group discussion on cancel events.

There is an excellent discussion in which practitioners like yourself discuss the application of cancel events:

https://groups.google.com/forum/#!topic/BPMNforum/UIEasgrpfY4

Meditating Mike
Collaborating with BPMN Practitioners

After you have read the forum discussion, take a moment and think about how you would answer the practitioner's question.

From your experience so far, does it make sense to use a cancel event in the instance described? Additionally, ask yourself, what follow-up questions would you ask the practitioner if you could?

For us, we would ask what type of subprocess they are trying to depict. We would also ask the nature of the event that they are trying to describe. A lot of times with BPMN and building process models, taking a moment to think about what is being said during interview sessions enables us to ask clarifying questions that will determine what type of event is truly occurring and a proper way to depict it on the model.

4.1.3.3.7 Escalation Events

The *escalation event* is used to elevate key information to parent-level processes. Basically, it escalates a problem or issue without disrupting the subprocess. When applied, the escalation shows where in the process the event could occur. The BPMN language is allowing you to surface a business problem that occurs at a lower level but needs to be escalated to the parent process.

The escalation event has several characteristics:

- Can be start, intermediate, and end events

- Can be noninterrupting start and noninterrupting intermediate events

- Employs *throw-and-catch* concept

- Can have the *cancelActivity* attribute, but it is not the default

- Can be used to start an event subprocess

- Requires word matching for the throw and catch: If I use one word on the *throw* black escalation event, I have to use the same word for the *catch* white escalation event.

Let's explore the escalation event.

We often leverage enterprise architecture with BPM initiatives. The following model depicts the high-level processes for an enterprise architecture project. We use the escalation noninterrupting boundary event to depict that a catch is received notifying us of a delay in our architecture delivery. When the *escalating event* is triggered, a second sequence flow is generated, and we brief our customers regarding the delay. The processes still continue as normal; nothing is canceled or terminated. Executives are just made aware of a delay in schedule.

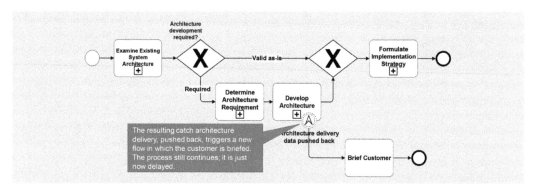

Figure 156: Identifying Escalation Boundary Events for Enterprise Architecture Processes

As we drill down into the subprocess for *Develop Architecture*, we will see the steps needed for developing an architecture. If the subject matter experts are unavailable, however, we are able to use the escalation *throw* event to depict a delay in architecture delivery. Some modelers would use a *timer event* to model this situation. While the word *delay* implies the concept of time, it is not the proper modeling construct for this situation. The escalation event throws that delay notification to the parent process to trigger an *exception flow*. The timer event would not do the throw. The key is both the subprocess and the parent process continue. So, as the escalation event occurs in the subprocess, an exception flow leads to another activity that occurs in the parent process.

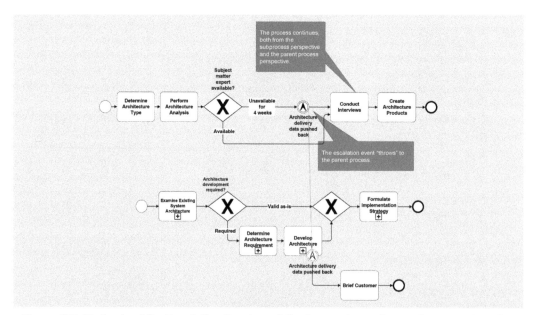

Figure 157: Understand the Escalation Events and the Connection to Parent Process—Develop Architecture

Meditating Mike
Reflecting on Your Organization's Influence on the Notation Patterns You Use

Are you resigned to the fact that you are going to break some of the rules of BPMN? What I mean by this is, are you striving for readability and translatability to a layperson's perspective or syntactically correct models?

Think about how your organization influences the notations you use. How do you strive for syntactically correct models and proper modeling techniques for some of these complex notations? Can you maintain a healthy balance of notations that won't overwhelm average readers? Let's illustrate how you can apply escalation events in a way you can reach the layperson.

General Practitioner
Escalating Your Understanding of BPMN

Don't let the concept of escalation prohibit you from modeling syntactically correct models. When applied effectively, it can be taught to anyone.

Online shopping is all the rage. We particularly love the quick delivery of goods. But who has ordered something with a two-day delivery only to receive a delay notification? It's pretty common for people living in the Midwest. Let's take a moment and model this situation, applying escalation events to the shipping process. Let's start by building out the following *Transport Cargo* subprocess details for when a customer orders something online. Recreate the following model.

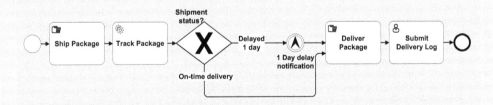

Figure 158: Applying Escalation Events to the Delivery Process

Now, look at the following *tactical process* describing an organization's unique steps and apply the escalation event for one-day delay notification. Specifically, apply the *escalation event* and describe the following steps:

- If a delay occurs, additional steps are taken to *notify customers* of a delay.

- The tracking systems generate an automated notification *updating the delivery status* which is sent to the customer via preferred contact method.

• After all monthly status reports are collected, management executes a new set of activities for evaluating shipping delays.

Based on your understanding of escalation events, apply these steps to the following tactical process.

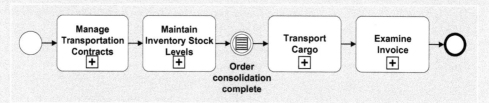

Figure 159: Tactical Process Model for Escalation Exercise

The following shows how we modeled the escalation exercise. We used the *noninterrupting escalation boundary event* with the one-day delay notification. We used the *service task* to illustrate how the system updates delivery status for a delay. Additionally, for context, we added a *customer pool*, demonstrating how an alert goes out for the updated delivery notification. We apply the *conditional event* to illustrate that monthly status reports are collected so that we can begin to evaluate shipping delays. We depict *evaluate shipping delays* as a *collapsed subprocess* because, in the previous criteria we stated, a new set of activities begins. Since we did not define the steps, we used the collapsed subprocess.

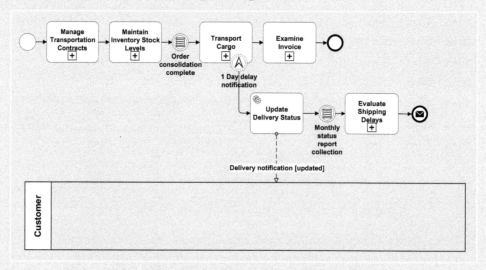

Figure 160: A Solution for the Escalation Exercise

Why did you use the conditional event for the monthly status report collection and not a timer event?

The timer event sounds tempting to apply when you hear *monthly*, right? The reason why we did not use the timer event was the qualifier *monthly status report collection*. Even though it is the end of the month or beginning of a new month, until the event *monthly status report collection* occurs for monthly reports, our process waits. In that instance, the conditional event was appropriate.

Hopefully, throughout this section, we have expanded your understanding of events and boundary events. More importantly, we hope that your application of these concepts has made a connection with you as you have built and applied these concepts.

As with many of these chapters, we struggled to determine what to include and what to exclude regarding exercises and examples. When we finished this book, we had so many different real-world experiences that it was impossible to include them all. For instance, we didn't include examples of multiple and parallel multiple events used on the boundary of an activity. However, for those who want more, you are in luck! Join us at our website as we provide additional training material and examples that will continue your learning experience with BPMN.

4.1.4 Advanced Gateways and Sequence Flows

Are you ready to start examining the complexity of BPMN? If you have made it this far, we think you are. We have pulled back several layers of BPMN through an examination of events and the token concept. Now, in this section, we will examine the remaining *sequence flows* and *gateways*.

You might be asking yourself, why didn't they just teach all of the gateways in chapter 3? To be honest, it's a fair question. Our approach to learning BPMN is that the further you get in modeling complex organizational processes, the more complex the set of notations you'll need. We believe it is unfair to bombard you with notations that you may not need if you are just trying to learn the basic modeling technique. Had we included every gateway at the start, chapter 3 would have ended up being too long, and the new BPMN modeler could have felt overwhelmed. Worse, a new BPMN modeler could have taken an advanced notation and attempted to apply it when it wasn't required.

With that, let's begin by discussing *inclusive gateways* and *conditional* and *default sequence flow* notations.

4.1.4.1 Inclusive Gateways and Conditional and Default Sequence Flows

In this section, we discuss the *inclusive gateway* or the OR gateway. (We will get into the OR shortly.) We will start by explaining the inclusive gateway and provide some key points to help understand how to model with this gateway. Then we will dive into the *conditional* and *default* sequence flows. As practitioners, we felt saving these two sequence flows for the inclusive gateway makes sense and after our discussion, we hope it makes sense to you.

The inclusive gateway has several characteristics:

- Displayed as a gateway with an *O* in the middle

- For each *true* condition, the process path is taken; this means at least one (or multiple) paths can be taken.

- Data-driven gateway

We will use a simple model to explain the inclusive gateway. The inclusive gateway allows you to model a data-driven decision for one or more paths. In the following model, we evaluate our training material. Depending on the need, we determine whether to update video resources, PowerPoint resources, our lecture transcripts, or a combination of the three. The inclusive gateway allows us to model taking one or more of these paths. We could take one path, two, or three. It really depends on the expressions we define as the process path. The inclusive gateways give us that modeling power. But with great power comes the possibility of great complexity.

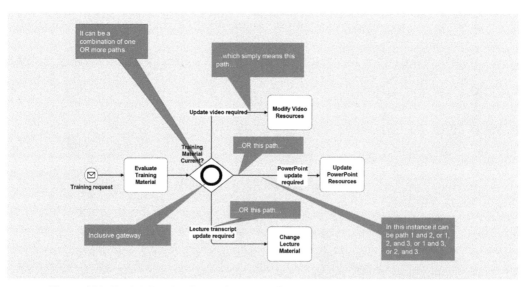

Figure 161: Explaining the OR for Inclusive Gateways—Manage Training Material

As with the parallel gateway and exclusive gateway, the *inclusive gateway* has merge, or *synchronizing*, characteristics. The synchronizing characteristics can be depicted using Trisotech modeler in the following two models. In the first illustration, we show the first token arriving at the synchronizing inclusive gateway. In this case, we want to model waiting for the second token that is still active.

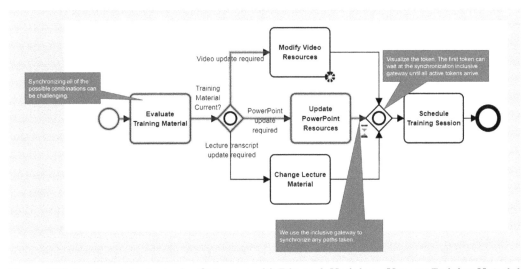

Figure 162: Synchronizing Inclusive Gateways with Trisotech Modeler—Manage Training Material

After all expected sequence flows arrive, the inclusive gateway synchronizes our process and we can move to the next activity and schedule training sessions.

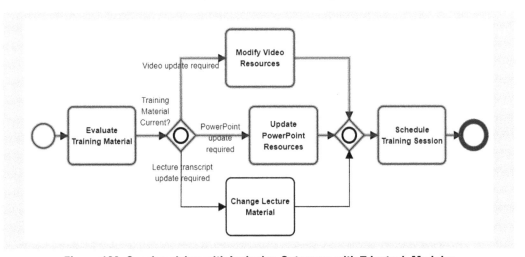

Figure 163: Synchronizing with Inclusive Gateways with Trisotech Modeler

General Practitioner
Experience Turning Interview Notes into a Business Process Model Using Inclusive Gateways

Build, build, build with those inclusive gateways or your model will never get done.

Conducting interviews is a great way of capturing the process from the subject matter expert's (SME) perspective. While we have found that we love to model on the spot with experts, at times we send an interview questionnaire before the modeling session to get some basic information. Use the following interview response example to build a business process model using inclusive gateways.

The following is an excerpt from an interview about transportation movements. For readability, we highlighted key information, similar to what we would do with any interview response.

> "Our process begins with a receipt of an order for movement. The planner reviews the order and *determines the movement requirement.* Depending on the determination, the planner has some options. The planner can *select an air carrier,* **or** *select a rail carrier,* **or** *select a truck carrier,* **or** a *combination* of these options depending on the shipment. While selecting the mode, in **parallel,** the planner *verifies transportation account codes.* After the mode selection has been made **and** the account codes have been verified, the planner *books selected options.* The process ends with a message being sent to the selected carriers."

Before you move any further or look at the possible solution depicted in the following model, take a moment and try to *build a model* based on these interview notes. Often, we must rely on our own understanding of SME details to create that initial model. After you have completed your model, take a look at our solution. How close were you to our modeling? How was your model different? Join us on our forums to share and discuss.

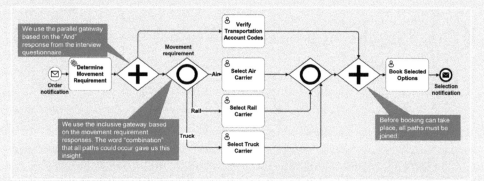

Figure 164: Turning Interview Notes into a Business Process Model Using Inclusive Gateways—Possible Solution

Forum Felicia

Multiple Gateway Type Discussion *Contributing to the BPMN Practitioner community can help facilitate the transfer of knowledge. Forum groups and discussion boards with questions provide us that opportunity.*

At the time of writing this book, there was a great unanswered question regarding the use of multiple exclusive gateways following inclusive gateways. Take a moment and review the question at hand. Can you answer the BPMN practitioners question?

https://groups.google.com/forum/#!topic/BPMNforum/mOpUhv8AplE

Now that you have reflected on the forum question and shed light on modeling challenges with gateways let's expand on the application of the inclusive gateway by introducing the default sequence flow and conditional sequence flow.

4.1.4.1.1 Default Sequence Flows and Conditional Sequence Flows

Up until this point, we have only been using the *normal flow* or *uncontrolled sequence flow* notation while modeling our processes. In this section, we describe the default sequence flow and *conditional sequence flow*.

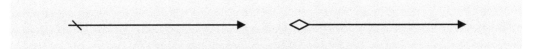

Figure 165: Default and Conditional Sequence Flow

The default sequence flow has several characteristics:

- Is depicted with a slash at the beginning of the sequence flow.

- *Default* means the path will be taken if the other sequence flow conditions are set to *false*

- Used for data-driven *exclusive* or *inclusive gateways*

- *Activities* and *complex gateways* can be the source that defines a default sequence flow

- Can be used to show the *default process flow*

- Can be used when multiple sequence flows are directly out of an activity (no gateway)

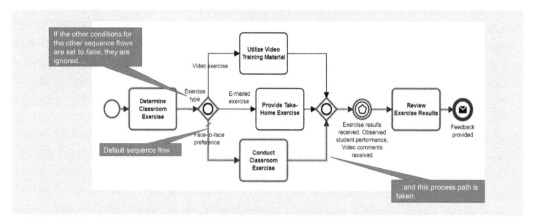

Figure 166: Default Sequence Flow using Trisotech Modeler

The *conditional sequence flow* must meet certain criteria for the sequence flow to be activated.

The conditional sequence flow has several characteristics:

- Depicted with a diamond at the beginning of the sequence flow

- Used to depict *conditional expressions*, meaning we can use conditional sequence flows in place of *inclusive gateways*

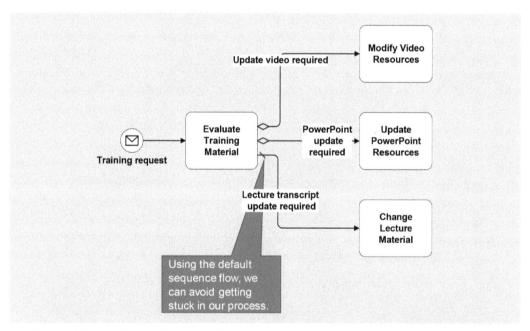

Figure 167: Conditional Sequence Flow Example—An Alternative to Inclusive Gateways

Keep in mind that you use *default* and *conditional sequence flows* in combination. We illustrate how one can get stuck in the following model. In this case, we depicted each sequence flow as *conditional*. If none of the conditions were set to *true*, then the process would be stuck. Using the *default sequence flow* would prevent your process from being stuck.

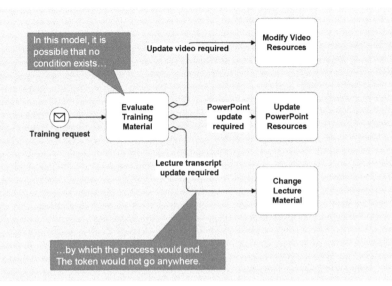

Figure 168: Avoid Getting Stuck with Conditional Sequence Flows

Forum Felicia
Adding to the Body of BPMN Practitioner Knowledge

There is a great discussion happening right now regarding sequence flows and gateways.

As you read the various BPMN practitioners' comments, try to add something based on your experience and perspective of sequence flows:

https://groups.google.com/forum/#!topic/BPMNforum/ozGF3-q0uFQ

Surfer Dave Pro Tip

I hope my surfer jargon has not confused my BPMN expressions. Expressions come in two forms. Hopefully, my expressions based on natural-language text are understandable.

That's right: expressions come in two forms. The first form is *underspecified expressions*, meaning they are not executable and are written in a *natural-language text*. We only use natural-language text during this book for our sequence flow expressions. The second expression form is *executable expressions* or *formal expressions*. To execute formal expressions, we need an executable language specified in a *Uniform Resource Identifier format*. Join us on the forums to see our examples of *executable formal expressions*.

4.1.4.2 Event-Based Gateways

The gateways we have discussed so far have been largely based on data-driven decisions associated with the activity before the gateways. In this section, we describe the event-based gateway and how a future *event* determines the flow of the process. Event-based gateways enable us to model multiple *sequence flows* based on events that can occur.

The event-based gateway has several characteristics:

- Represented by a diamond and double circle (think multiple *intermediate events* inside a *gateway*)

- The process path *branching* is based on *events* that occur after the *gateway*.

- A specific *event* that occurs decides the *path* taken.

- Two or more *outbound sequence flows* required

- Can only use *message, signal*, timer, conditional, and *multiple* after an *event-based gateway*

- Can use *receive tasks* (discussed in detail in the following section)

So, let's teach the *event-based gateway* concept through the development and explanation of the following model.

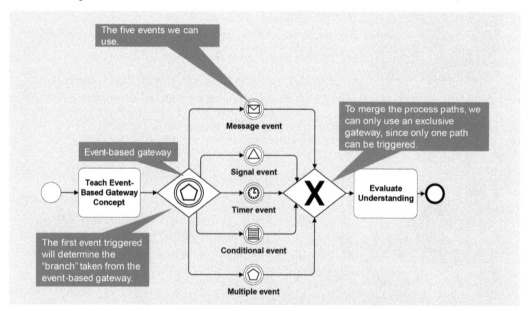

Figure 169: Teaching the Event-Based Gateway

Let's dive a little deeper into how to apply the event-based gateway. Within our enterprise operations, we have a *purchasing department* responsible for procuring material. It provides an opportunity to show the power of the event-based gateway through the purchasing process. Like most of the processes used in these examples, we simplify it. The following model depicts the application of the event-based gateway.

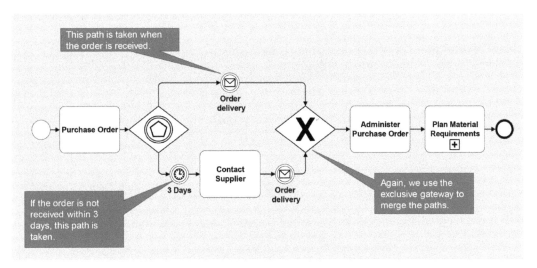

Figure 170: Analyzing the Event-Based Gateway for the Ordering Process

The purchasing department creates *purchase orders* (supplies, material, equipment, etc.) for a department in our enterprise. We use the *event-based gateway* to show that the order should be delivered, but after three days, if it is not received, we contact the supplier. If the order is delivered within three days, however, we take the top path. Regardless of which path is taken, the order has to be received before we can *administer the purchase order*.

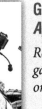

General Practitioner
Application of Event-Based Gateways

Remember, it's all about the events after the event-based gateway. Those events decide the process path taken based on which one occurs first.

All right. Now that we have described how to model with event-based gateways, let's create a BPMN model. In the following example, we depict a *simple shopping process*. We depict collaboration with an online retailer using the message *catch* and *throw* for starting and ending the process. We use the *event-based gateway* to depict how two events can determine the next steps in our process.

When the online retailer updates inventory, we can *buy more items*. We use the *signal event* to illustrate we will only *buy more items* if we see the *update* from the online retailer. But if we reach our purchase limit of $500 before new items are seen, we *purchase* the items and complete our process.

The key takeaway is that the first *conditional event* to occur controls the process path we take. That is the beauty of event-based gateways. The path taken is not based on data-driven decisions from previous steps; rather, it is driven by future events.

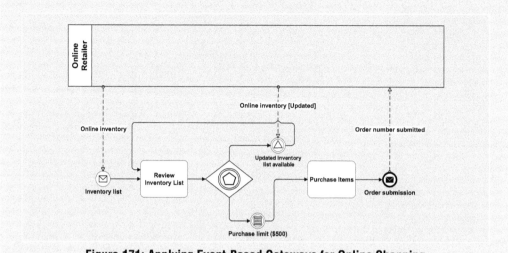

Figure 171: Applying Event-Based Gateways for Online Shopping

 **Streamer Seth** has created a video to improve your understanding of event-based gateways. Join Seth as he describes the application of event-based gateways: specifically, *how to use event-based gateways* as a mechanism for modeling complex processes and how you can *apply event-based gateways* to model out your complex processes.

Join us at https://www.bpmpractitioners.com/videos. The videos match the figure name. You can also view our YouTube channel, *Joshua Fuehrer.*

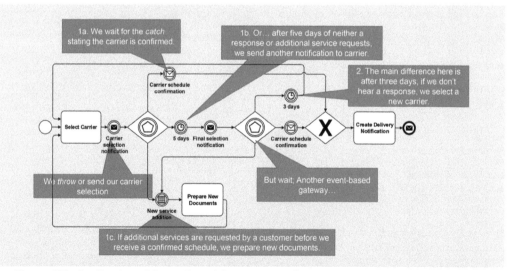

Figure 172: Application of Event-Based Gateways for Selecting Carriers for Transportation

Forum Felicia
Multiple Exclusive Events Discussion

What's that you say? You are ready to take your understanding of event-based gateways further?

Join the conversation on the application of event-based gateways. Here there is an interesting discussion on how to use timer events for an event-based gateway:

https://groups.google.com/forum/#!topic/BPMNforum/ZLywIozxtrg

Meditating Mike
Team Reflection for Event-Based Gateways

Having a collective debate within a team construct helps many people understand a notation more because, in that environment, everyone can share insights they did not have that other teammates may have, and vice versa.

Taking time to reflect as a team can help improve your understanding of a notation. Do you have the concept of the event-based gateway mastered, or are there things you don't fully understand? We highly encourage you to take time to discuss it with your team. The following is a narrative reflection exercise that you can apply to any experience. For this reflection exercise, focus on event-based gateways.

1. Reflect on a process modeling learning experience in which you felt satisfied.

2. Answer the following questions (write or type) in a narrative format:

   a. What experiences did you value while learning the specific notation?

   b. Describe your learning experience. Specifically, please describe anything that made it easier to learn the specific notation.

3. After you have responded, take a moment to examine your experience: How can you share those learning experiences with your colleagues?

Sharing those reflections and coming to a better understanding will improve the application of event-based gateways for your process models. Simply put, sharing your reflection from personal experience helps inform how you can apply BPMN. Taking time to discuss what worked for you will enable others to see a new perspective for learning a specific notation.

If you don't have a team to share, that's OK. You can join our forum discussion and share.

4.1.4.3 Process Instantiation with Event-Based and Parallel Gateways

Only two gateways can be used to start a process: the *event-based instantiation gateway* and the *parallel instantiation gateway*. In this section, we describe both.

We saved these gateways for last because both have exceptions to the earlier rules we stated. We hope that by now, you have modeled enough examples and have grasped the basic rules for sequence flows. To keep things simple earlier on, we said that gateways must have an *inbound sequence flow*. This is typically true; the exception is with *process instantiation using event-based or parallel gateways,* as there are no inbound sequence flows.

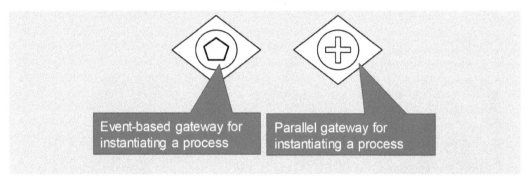

Figure 173: Depiction of Process Instantiation Gateways—Event-Based and Parallel

4.1.4.3.1 Instantiating the Process with Event-Based Gateways

Like the event-based gateways described in the previous section, the instantiation of a process with an event-based gateway has similar characteristics. The main difference is that the gateway is used to start a process based on the events that occur *after* the gateway.

The process instantiation event-based gateway has several characteristics:

- Process path *branching* based on the events that occur

- Specific *event* governs the path taken

- Represented by a diamond and one circle (think *multiple start event*) inside a *gateway*

- Two or more *outbound sequence flows* required

- No inbound *sequence flow* (treat it like a *start event*)

- Can only use *message, signal, timer, conditional,* and *multiple* after an event-based gateway

Let's depict how we can use the event-based gateway to instantiate a process. The following example illustrates the event-based gateway instantiating a process.

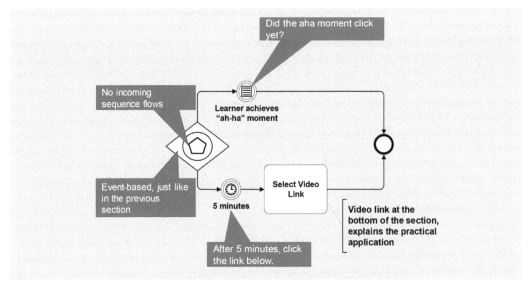

Figure 174: Teaching Instantiation—Event-Based Gateway

If we were able to make a connection based on your previous experiences with event-based gateways, the *aha* moment should have occurred. If, after reading this text and looking at the illustration for five minutes, it doesn't quite make the connection for you, go to the following video link. There we describe process instantiation with event-based gateways a bit further.

Want to see event-based gateways in action for starting a process? Join **Streamer Seth** as he explains how to model with event-based gateways and how you can use them to start your process.

Join us at https://www.bpmpractitioners.com/videos.

The videos match the figure name. You can also view our YouTube channel, *Joshua Fuehrer.*

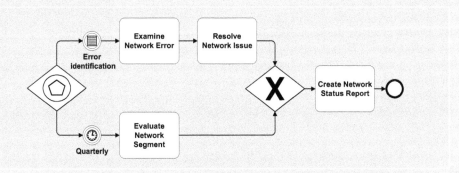

Figure 175: Streamer Seth's Process Instantiation with Event-Based Gateways

4.1.4.3.1 Instantiating the Process with Parallel Gateways

Process instantiation can also be depicted using parallel gateways. The main difference between the parallel gateway and event-based gateway when instantiating a process is that *all events* listed after the parallel gateway *must occur.*

The process instantiation parallel gateway has several characteristics:

- The *first event triggered* instantiates the process.

- Other events listed *wait to be triggered* before the normal process is completed.

- Can only use *message, signal, timer, conditional,* and *multiple* after an instantiation parallel gateway

- All events listed after the parallel gateway instantiation must occur (at some point).

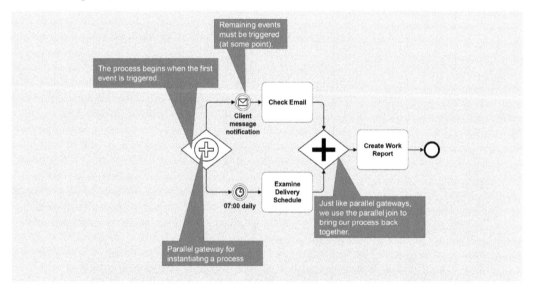

Figure 176: Examining Process Instantiation with Parallel Gateways

To help illustrate process instantiation, we will use Trisotech modeler to show the *manage financial records* process. The following model illustrates how process instantiation occurs. When we receive a payment notification, the process begins. You will notice that the timer event waits until 7:00 a.m. daily. In the meantime, our system is *processing payments, validating charges,* and *filing expense reports.* It is not until 7:00 a.m. that we log in and the other process path is taken.

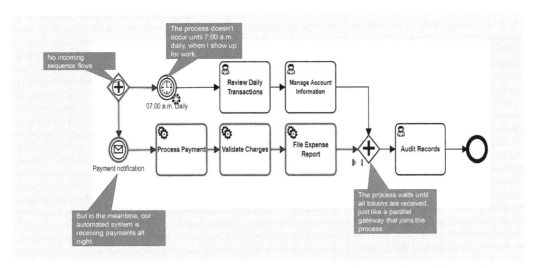

Figure 177: Process Instantiation with Parallel Gateway—Manage Financial Records

Like the parallel *join*, the first token waits until the second token arrives at the synchronizing parallel gateway before we move on to *audit records*.

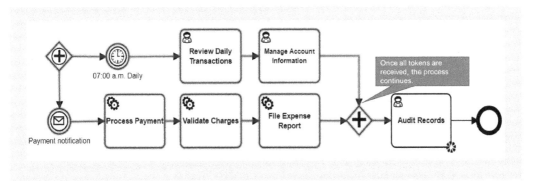

Figure 178: Merging a Process Instantiation with Parallel Gateway—Manage Financial Records

General Practitioner
Experience Evaluating Process Behavior for Instantiating Your Process with Parallel Gateways

Going and applying what we just heard is the biggest step for learning, and it is the way we get the most out of the experience. To validate our understanding, we should have someone review our model and provide meaningful feedback. That is very important.

Validation is crucial to BPMN, not only from a process model perspective but from a learning perspective. To demonstrate, let's explore process instantiation using parallel gateways in the following stock management process exercise.

The first event triggered will start the process: in this instance, *negative change in held stocks* occurs first. The other two events will wait until those triggering events occur.

What would happen if the market crashes and it is only 8:00 a.m.?

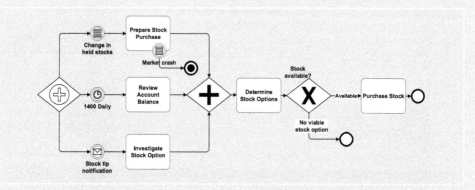

Figure 179: Understanding Exceptions of Instantiating with Parallel Gateways

Answer: All of the remaining tokens, events, and activities would be *terminated*. We know for sure that the event *14:00 daily* hasn't been triggered because it is only 8:00 a.m. when the market crashed, so that event is terminated.

Now, let's examine a new instance of our process. What would have happened if the event *stock tip received* was triggered first? What would happen if the market crash occurred later in the day?

Answer: We would terminate any remaining tokens, events, and activities since we are still waiting on all the tokens to synchronize at the parallel gateway.

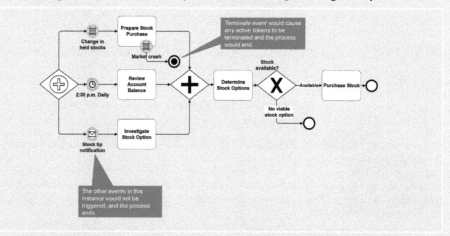

Figure 180: Solution for Exceptions of Instantiating with Parallel Gateways

Did your previous experience and the examples in this book enable you to answer this question correctly? Did the validation we provided help you to feel more comfortable about instantiating processes with parallel gateways?

4.1.4.4 Complex Gateways

Complex gateways are designed to deal with complicated business rules. Before you pass over this section because we used the word complex, let's rephrase: it's the *behavior* associated with the gateway that some find difficult.

Complex gateways are used to model *unique processes with complex behaviors*. While the other gateways we have covered can handle almost every modeling situation, complex gateways are used to handle what parallel, event-based, and inclusive gateways cannot. In this section, we describe a few ways you can model complex behaviors.

The complex gateway has several characteristics:

- Always in one of two states: *waiting to start* or *waiting for reset,* meaning when a token arrives, the process flow may continue

- Based on a Boolean instance attribute:

  – *waitingForStart* or *waitingForReset*

    > *Reminder:* Boolean values are usually defined by *true* or *false*. So, if our *waitingForStart* is set *true*, then we are waiting for a token to activate the complex gateway.

- Sequence flows must have *expressions* that indicate which path is taken and needed to *activate* the gateway, meaning not all process paths are required to start the gateway.

- Basically, the process flow may continue without all of the outstanding tokens at the gateway.

Let's look at how we can model with complex gateways in the following shopping example. We begin by completing our shopping list. In parallel, we search online with our mobile device while we visit our local mall. We want to complete either purchase whenever we are ready to do so. We can model this behavior with a complex gateway; the following model depicts purchasing gifts.

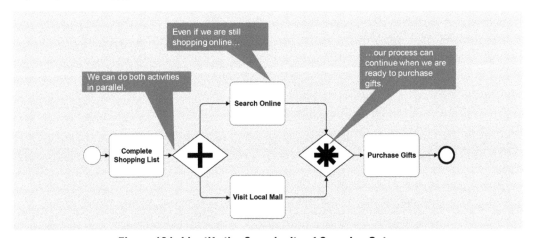

Figure 181: Identify the Complexity of Complex Gateways

Let's share another example using complex gateways. The following model depicts how we learn BPMN and how one might start building process models after learning BPMN. After establishing learning goals, our organization has a set of steps for helping new employees learn BPMN. We *attend online courses, complete an in-person seminar, read the BPMN specification*, and *complete a peer review session*. While we don't do all of this at once, we can use the complex gateway to illustrate that *once two types of training modes are completed*, our process can continue, and we can start developing process models.

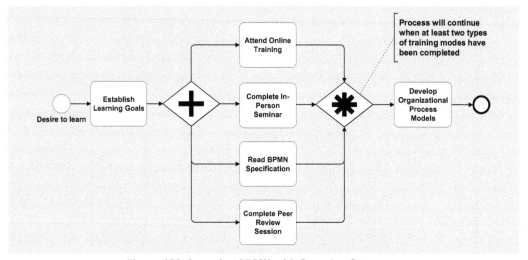

Figure 182: Learning BPMN with Complex Gateways

General Practitioner
Complex Gateway Application for Employee Performance Evaluations

I hope they don't evaluate my complex nature. I just really love dressing in old-fashioned military attire.

Modeling the complex gateway can be pretty straightforward when you understand conditions. Let's apply the complex gateway to performance reporting—something most of us, either as supervisors or employees, have experienced.

Let's begin by identifying the steps in the process:

1. As the first activity, the manager evaluates performance reports.

2. Use the *inclusive gateway* to depict that two paths can be taken based on the *true* conditions.

   a. In this case, it can be true that there are *poorly written assessments* and *individual issues:* Use *two sequence flows* from the inclusive gateway.

   b. If both are *true*, both paths are taken, and we execute each activity.

3. After *poorly written assessments*, the first activity is a collapsed subprocess, *conduct training*.

4. After *individual issues*, the first activity is *interview employee* (user task).

5. We use the complex gateway to illustrate joining our process flow back together. The process continues when data is available (use *text annotation*).

6. The first activity after the complex gateway is *collect operational data*.

7. We use the *conditional intermediate event* to depict that our process won't continue until all the *data is collected*.

8. Once all data has been collected, we synthesize our findings.

In the following figure, we depict a complex gateway to illustrate that when the *token* arrives from the *interview employee* activity, the process can continue and we can *collect operational data*. To prevent us from *synthesizing findings* before our conduct training is completed, however, we use a *conditional intermediate event* to illustrate that *all data has been collected* before we can continue in our process.

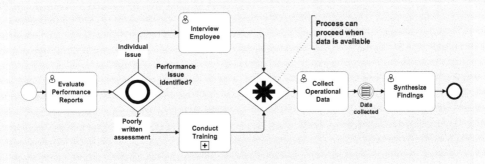

Figure 183: Building with the Complex Gateway

Meditating Mike
The Complex Nature of Sustained Reflection

Let's take a moment and reflect on complex gateways: specifically, how your behaviors influence your learning.

Let's take a minute and reflect on the complexity of behaviors that influence learning.

1. Can you describe any internal driving forces that influenced your learning process?

2. Can you describe any positive learning experiences that influenced your understanding of BPMN?

As you reflect on those questions, take a moment and write down your answers. We would love to hear from you regarding how you responded. If you have time, join us in our forum discussion and share your previous experiences.

Forum Felicia
Complex Experiences from a BPMN Practitioner's Lens

There is an interesting discussion on complex gateways that I highly recommend you check out. As you read through the various responses, ask yourself: Do I face similar challenges in my understanding of the complexity of BPMN?"

If you answered yes, you are not alone. BPMN practitioners range in experience and knowledge, and that's OK. You are striving to learn the best ways to leverage the expertise around you and continue to build on your knowledge of BPMN.

https://groups.google.com/forum/#!topic/BPMNforum/2hfs5Ft5-_s

4.1.5 Expanding the Application of BPMN Activities and Subprocesses

Now let's continue expanding the use of BPMN by applying remaining BPMN activities. This will allow us to start accounting for very complex or technical process models. In this section, we illustrate how you can apply the remaining *subprocesses*, *task markers*, and *task types* to improve your understanding of BPMN.

4.1.5.1 Event Subprocesses

Have you ever wondered why we are so restricted in the event types we can use for regular subprocesses? This is because of the *event subprocess*.

In this section, we describe the event subprocess and expand on the use of the *types of start events* we can use. Event subprocesses are unique in that they are instantiated based on a *triggered start event*. As a reminder, the normal subprocesses we have modeled thus far are instantiated when a *normal control flow* (*sequence flow*) triggers the subprocess.

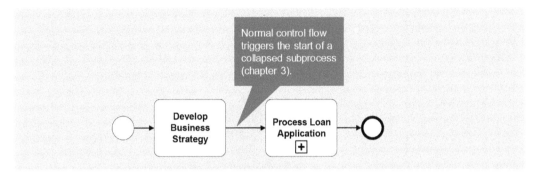

Figure 184: Normal Control Flow Triggering a Collapsed Subprocess

The event subprocess has several characteristics:

- Not part of a parent process: encapsulated within subprocesses

- No incoming or outgoing sequence flows

- Can occur while a parent process is active, except when used for compensation (*See the bullet statement below concerning compensation.*)

  - Triggered by *events*, whereas normal subprocesses are triggered via *sequence flows*.

- To trigger an event subprocess, the event must be defined, meaning only certain types of events can be used: *message, error, escalation, compensation, timer, signal, conditional, parallel multiple,* and *multiple.* (In the following illustration, we depict interrupting, and noninterrupting event collapsed subprocesses.)

  - Compensation events can only be triggered in event subprocesses after the parent process in which an event subprocess resides is completed.

- Can only have one start event

- Depicted with dotted lines

- Can be depicted a *collapsed* or *expanded* subprocess

- Collapsed subprocesses depict the start event in the upper left corner.

The following are illustrations of the collapsed and expanded subprocesses using various tools.

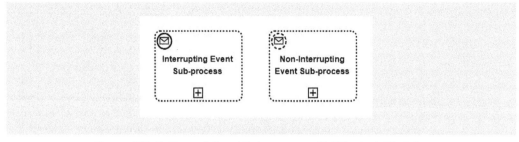

Figure 185: Collapsed Event Subprocess with Trisotech Modeler

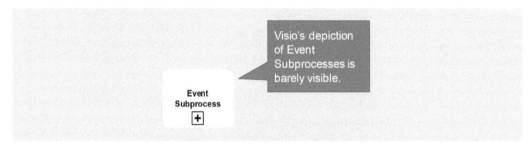

Figure 186: Collapsed Event Subprocess with Visio

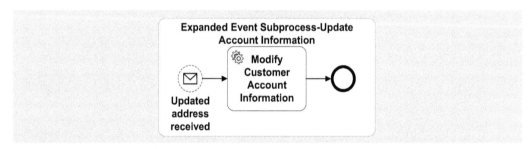

Figure 187: Expanded Event Subprocess

An important note: event subprocesses can also be started by *interrupting start events*. That's right. There are *two ways* to start event subprocesses and *two different outcomes*.

In the following illustration, we expand out our process to illustrate how two different event subprocesses can be initiated within the context of an expanded subprocess. In the expanded subprocess for processing loan applications, we have depicted a set of activities.

We also depict two different *event subprocesses*. The first one looks familiar: it's *update account information*. When updated address information is received, a *noninterrupting message start event* starts the event subprocess for updating your address for your account. After the account information is updated, the event subprocess ends.

The second event subprocess is different, as we use an *interrupting conditional start event* to illustrate when the condition *account closed* triggers the start of the process: we close the customer account. The key thing to highlight is the *event type* that we used to start our event subprocess. The *interrupting event subprocess* interrupts the *parent process* for *process loan application*. We use a *boundary message event* to express that an exception occurs and a new process, m*anage customer service*, is completed.

You will notice because we are using Visio, we use a gray fill-in for the expanded subprocess so you can see the event subprocess notation.

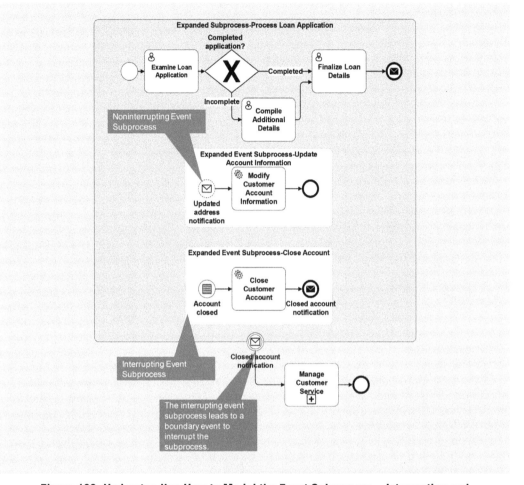

Figure 188: Understanding How to Model the Event Subprocess—Interrupting and Noninterrupting Event Subprocesses

Streamer Seth has created a video on how you can leverage the event subprocess notation when modeling.

Join us at https://www.bpmpractitioners.com/videos.

The videos match the figure name. You can also view our YouTube channel, *Joshua Fuehrer.*

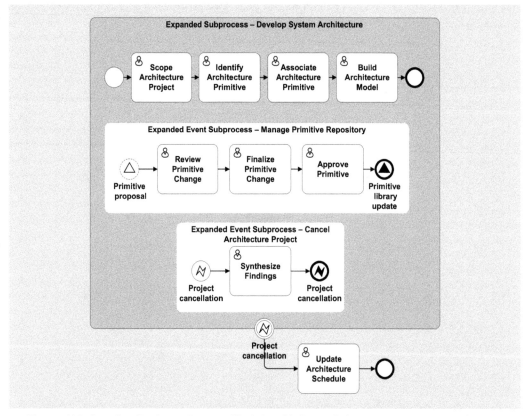

Figure 189: Creating Business Process Models with Event Subprocesses—Develop System Architecture

While Visio doesn't allow you to illustrate the event in the upper-left corner, other modeling tools enable the proper depiction.

The following example shows the *event types* that trigger *event subprocesses*. For simplicity, we broke them out between interrupting and noninterrupting.

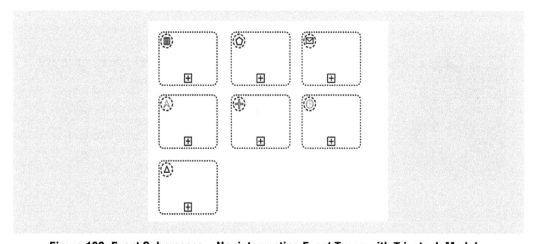

Figure 190: Event Subprocess—Noninterrupting Event Types with Trisotech Modeler

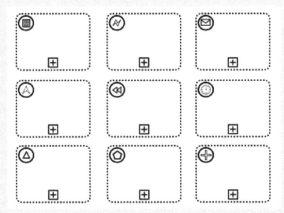

Figure 191: Event Subprocess—Interrupting Event Types with Trisotech Modeler

General Practitioner
Experience Leveraging Event Subprocesses to Create Detailed Models

Some notations aren't used by BPMN practitioners—not because they are difficult, but because there is limited information regarding how you can apply them effectively in your organization's business process models.

In the following example, we provide a case for how you can apply noninterrupting event type notations. These notations will add to your modeling notation subset. By understanding how to apply them, you are more likely to see where they can be used for modeling initiatives.

Let's try the following exercise. The text for each process will be described by color coding.

- The green text describes the happy-day path
- The *red text* describes an event subprocess that is interrupting
- The blue text describes an event-subprocess that is noninterrupting

The following describes an expanded subprocess for *Plan To-Be Projects.* The process begins, and the first activity is the allocation of project funds. The second activity, the planner, gathers requirements. After the activity ends, a message is sent to key players. In parallel, the following steps occur:

- When *additional details* are received, the planner will examine requirement details.
- The planner evaluates the project charter.
- The planner determines stakeholders.
- After all three activities are complete, the process merges and ends.

The first expanded event subprocess describes how to manage the fund's compensation process. The process began when a *fund rescinded* notification is received (**use a compensation start event**). The planner *modifies project account information*, removing funds tied to the account. The **expanded event-subprocess** process ends after funds are rescinded from project account (**use a compensation "throwing" intermediate event**). Use an error event to illustrate no funds.

- When a *funds rescinded notification* occurs, the throwing compensation event *throws* to the catch *funds rescinded notification* compensation event attached to the boundary of allocate project funds activity.

- The association flow from the boundary event leads to a compensation activity, *return project funds*. The activity undoes the allocation of funds and balances the account to appropriate levels.

- Additionally, since our event subprocess is interrupted, we use the *intermediate boundary error event* to illustrate an exception to our process, and we document our findings.

The second expanded event subprocess describes the following situation: when stakeholder information is received, the planner updates stakeholder details in the project system. The process ends with project details being updated with appropriate stakeholder information.

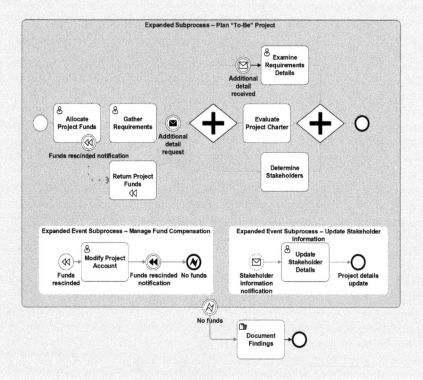

Figure 192: Possible Solution for Plan To-Be Projects

Let's examine the event subprocess possible solution. In the first event subprocess, we used compensation to start the event subprocess because we needed to illustrate how funds are rescinded in our process. As a reminder, compensation is used to undo a previously completed task, so in this instance, we are able to model the return of project funds only after the expanded subprocess is completed and a *fund rescinded* event occurs in the expanded event subprocess. The interrupting event subprocess, as the name implies, interrupts the happy-day process we modeled first; whereas, we used the noninterrupting event to start our second expanded event subprocess. We did so because our happy-day process isn't affected by the update of stakeholder information.

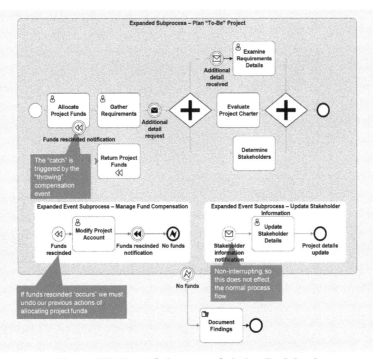

Figure 193: Event Subprocess Solution Explained

Forum Felicia
Online Discussion for Event Subprocesses

There is a great question and excellent responses regarding how to use event subprocesses on the forum. Let's take a break and check out current comments from BPMN practitioners. After you read the question and BPMN practitioner responses, ask yourself: Can I see other uses for the event subprocess?"

Go to: https://groups.google.com/forum/#!topic/BPMNforum/hlGtLh58Obs

The event subprocess is sometimes overlooked, but when you begin to understand the power it brings to modeling, you can start describing very complex processes. We dive a little more into modeling complex process models in the next chapter and illustrate how you can apply it to your organization.

4.1.5.2 Transaction Subprocesses

In this section, we will describe the unique nature of *transaction subprocesses* and how you can apply this notation to your organizational process models. The transaction subprocess is unique for BPMN in that it has a special behavior controlled by *transaction protocols*.

Transaction protocols are standards used for communication. Specifically, transaction protocols describe in detail the format of messages to ensure interoperability, security, and reliability for such communication. There are various types of transaction protocols, from *multipurpose transaction protocols* to *web service transaction protocols*.

Wait...hmm
a transaction
protocol?

The transaction subprocess has several characteristics:

- Must confirm *all participants* have completed the transaction before the happy-day path continues to the parent process from the *transaction subprocess*

- Depicted with double lines

- If the process is canceled, all of the activities within the transaction subprocess are canceled.

- Compensation can occur in a transaction subprocess.

- Three ways to illustrate the cancellation of a transaction subprocess:

  - *Cancel end event* at the end of the transaction subprocess

  - *Cancel intermediate event* attached to the subprocess boundary that contains a *cancel message*

  - *Error intermediate event* to represent a hazard, indicating something terribly wrong. Use the *error intermediate event* when a cancel event cannot cancel the activities during execution. The error intermediate event is connected to the boundary of the transaction subprocess, which generates a new exception flow.

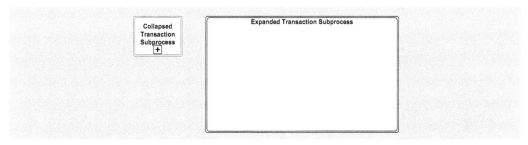

Figure 194: Depiction of Transaction Subprocess—Collapsed and Subprocess

To help illustrate transaction subprocesses, we use a process model called *Create BPMN Model* and then *Simulate Model*.

We start the process with a collapsed subprocess: *Create BPMN Model*. Upon completion of our BPMN model, we enter into a transaction expanded subprocess: *Simulate Model*. Now we can run a simulation of our model. The *as-is* version of the simulation will set our baseline, and after changes are made to the model, a *to-be* version can be run and differences analyzed. We added two different events to identify potential problems with our process. The first is an *error event* which indicates we have syntactical discrepancies. This would result in the transaction subprocess erroring out, and we would be forced to create, or at least modify, the BPMN model (organizational resources required to create or modify). We also added *cancel the event* for the second hazard that can occur. In this case, simulation failed to produce real outcomes.

Simulation can fail for many reasons: missing steps, incorrect input parameters, or an error in one of the equations. The failure results in a cancel event, which leads to another activity outside of the *transaction expanded subprocess* to submit a failure report.

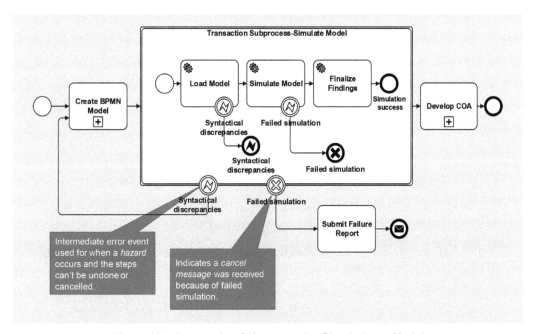

Figure 195: Transaction Subprocess for Simulating a Model

General Practitioner
Creating a Transaction Subprocess Exercise

If at first you don't succeed, try again. Look within and examine the reasons behind why you failed before trying again. Persistence during the learning process is very important to your success.

Now that we have covered the basics of the transaction subprocesses, let's create a BPMN model using the expanded transaction subprocess. In the following example, we provide you with the overarching process model describing how we handle our clients. The process begins when we receive a contract for a new client. We deliver a welcome package. After the client receives the welcome package, in parallel, we provide client services and manage client accounts. Both processes consist of multiple activities and must be complete before we end our process.

So, fill in and model the following steps within the expanded transaction subprocess.

- *Manage client account* expanded transaction subprocess consists of two activities:
  - *Process payments* and *deposit funds*
    - > *Process payments* must occur before we can *deposit funds*
  - If a client is dropped, we cancel the management of client accounts.
  - The cancellation leads us to update our company profile.

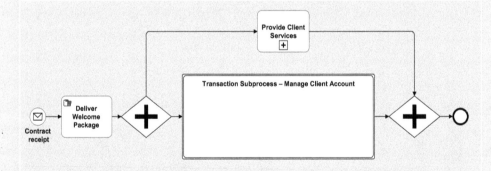

Figure 196: Transaction Subprocess Fill-in-the-Blank Exercise

Take a moment before looking ahead and fill in the blanks. Recreate the provided model and then apply your understanding of transaction subprocesses.

The following is our possible solution for modeling with transaction subprocesses.

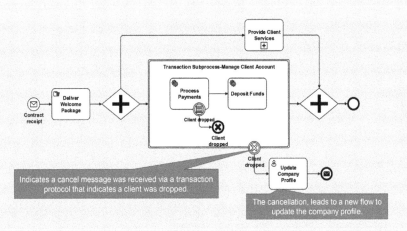

Figure 197: Possible Solution for Transaction Subprocess Fill-in-the-Blank Exercise

We used the sequence flow to illustrate that *process payments* is completed before *deposit funds*. Additionally, we illustrate that the *process is canceled* when a transaction protocol is received indicating a client has been dropped. We cancel the process of managing a client's account. Typically, several steps would occur after a client was dropped; for the sake of simplicity, we only show one—*update company profile* from the cancellation event.

Streamer Seth created a video to illustrate how you can apply key concepts of the transaction subprocess.

Join us at www.bpmpractitioners.com/videos. The videos match the figure name. You can also view our YouTube channel, *Joshua Fuehrer.*

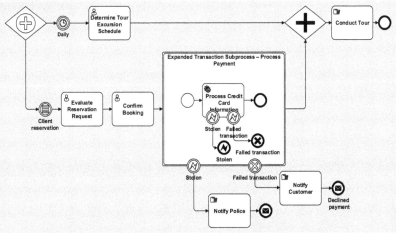

Figure 198: Streamer Seth Transaction Protocol Discussion

We encourage anyone who wants to know more about transaction subprocesses to join us on the forum and discuss your experiences with us. This is a great place to expand your understanding with other BPMN practitioners.

4.1.5.3 Calling the Global Process—Call Activity Expanded

In chapter 3, we described the *call activity*. Now we will dive into when call activities are used to call a *global process*.

Before we go on, let's discuss call activities again. Call activities are used to depict a point in the process at which a call is executed. A call activity can invoke either a *global task* or a *global process*. In either case, the *control is transferred* to the global task or process, the task is completed, and transfer of control then resumes in the main process.

In this section, we will discuss the nature of the global process. When a global *task* is called, it is only one task. When a global *process* is called, a process with multiple activities is invoked.

The following is an example of the global process collapsed subprocess and expanded subprocess for a global process.

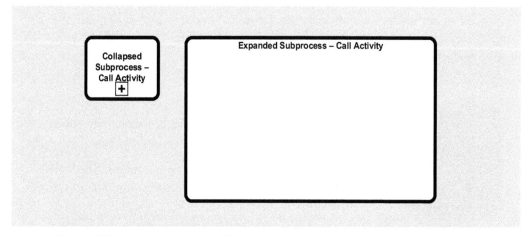

Figure 199: Representation of Callable Subprocesses—Collapsed and Expanded

The *call activity* to a global process has several characteristics:

- Represented as a bold line around the activity shape with a plus sign
- Represented by a bold line around the expanded subprocess notation
- Has unique data requirements it must fulfill
- Assumes control when invoked and returns control when the global process is completed

Let's expand on our earlier discussion regarding the data requirements that call activities must fulfill. In most process models, a transformation occurs through the completion of activities. Inputs are usually required, whether in the form of information or physical things. Those inputs are then transformed during the process, and an output results that represents that transformation. Call activities are great for showing us what we sent to another process and what we get in return; in essence, the output from the transformation of the other process.

Let's examine the following example of launching a new marketing strategy to illustrate what we mean. We *identify the new strategy* and then determine the availability of *marketing funds*. If we overspent and funds are unavailable, our process *transfers control to the finance department with a request for additional funds.*

Most modeling tools enable the option to display the data or keep it invisible. For this example, we illustrate how the data object *fund request, proposal* is the key data input to the global process. In the example, the global process illustrates the request for organizational resources. The first data output is in the form of *working capital approval notification*. We also depict a second data output, *denial letter*. Each is a unique output from the global process. While we don't know exactly what steps lead to these outputs, we know that there are two possible outputs. We use that data to complete our process because without a working capability approval notification or a denial letter, we cannot continue in executing the market strategy.

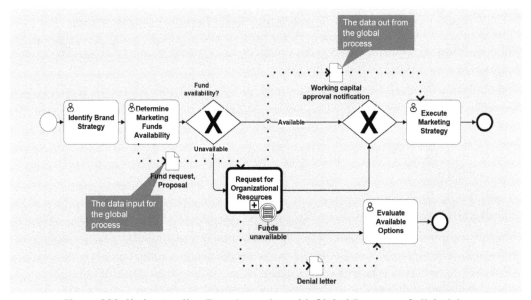

Figure 200: Understanding Transformation with Global Process—Call Activity

Let's expand the marketing process. We do this by using the expanded subprocess for a *global process notation* for the request for organizational resources. Doing so enables us to view another process within our organization.

We can see that the process starts by reviewing a request. We use a *boundary event* to illustrate when the condition *funds unavailable* occurs, a new process flow is generated, and this process ends.

If the conditional event is not set to *true*, however, or doesn't occur, the process continues with the allocation of funds and a notification that funds are approved. Now we can see why we used the *conditional intermediate boundary event*. It's because there are two possibilities in the global process. Each possibility will generate a different output. We illustrate process transformation of the global process by showing the data object outputs *working capability approval notification* and *denial letter*.

189

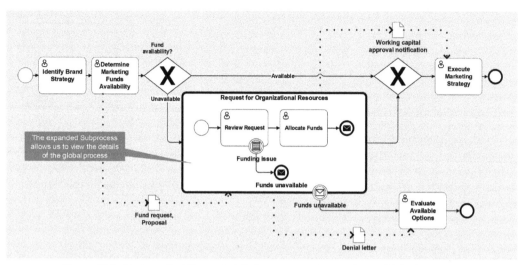

Figure 201: Portrayal of Expanded Subprocesses Executing a Global Process

The more complex your process model, the more likely using collapsed subprocesses will improve the readability and reduce the canvas size.

General Practitioner
Calling Global Processes Exercise

Let's practice creating a business process using global processes.

The following is an example of a fast food industry process; specifically, the administrative staff's process for evaluating the performance of various stores within a region. The process begins with a review of regional sales. The following model uses a *noninterrupting boundary event* to depict when targets are exceeded. A second new process flow that leads to our benchmark operation, depicted as a collapsed subprocess, is generated. We also assess operational conditions for those stores. We use the *inclusive gateway* to depict three paths from that assessment:

1. Workforce morale

2. Training deficiency

3. Scarcity issue

As a reminder, the inclusive gateway is used to depict that multiple paths can be taken based on the *true* conditions. We also depict the default sequence flow for scarcity issues, as that is typically the case for our process. If *workforce morale* and *training deficiency* are true, however, then our sequence flow leads to two different global processes. Again, we use the call activity notation and depict them as collapsed subprocesses.

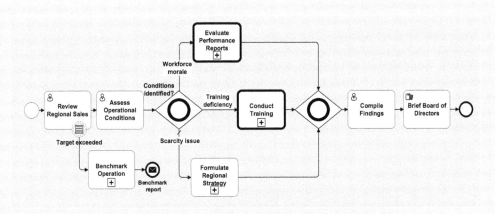

Figure 202: Demonstration of Global Processes in Action

If the two global processes are *called*, then process control is transferred, and we must wait for those two global processes to be completed before we can continue. That is because modeling with global processes, we provided an *input*, so, naturally, we expect output from those processes. The information created in those processes is important and requires examination within the context of our process.

Surfer Dave Pro Tip

Bro, I have a great idea for all of those BPMN practitioners out there not using a fancy modeling tool.

To help reduce the complexity of your process models, *text annotations* can display key pieces of information vital to understanding the process model and connect your organization's process models.

Let's model out Surfer Dave's Pro tip. In the following example, we use the text annotation to identify the resource role for the global process. Specifically, we identify the resource role for the activity that receives the data input. We also identify the resource role for the activity that sends us the data output.

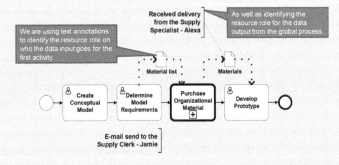

Figure 203: Surfer Dave Pro Tip—Identify Resource Roles for Global Processes

4.1.5.4 Ad-Hoc Subprocess

Ad-hoc subprocesses are unique; there is no specific process structure. The activities depicted do not proceed in any specific order unless specified through sequence flows. As we will see, ad-hoc subprocesses can be used to model human-driven processes. What that means is when determining which activities will be executed, a person is usually in charge of determining *which activities will be completed and when* to end the ad-hoc subprocess.

The ad-hoc subprocesses have several characteristics:

- Depicted with a *tilde symbol*
- Can be used in a *collapsed subprocess* or *expanded subprocess*
- Used to illustrate *no sequential relationships*
- The activities executed are determined by the performer (think person, role, etc.)
- Ad-hoc subprocess can complete without executing all of the activities.
- Can use *sequence flows* and *data flows* to identify dependencies
- May not use start event or end event

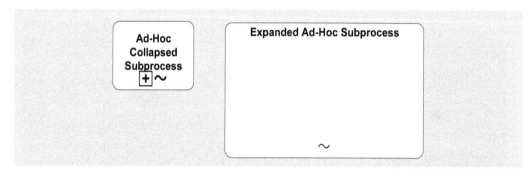

Figure 204: Ad-Hoc Collapsed and Expanded Subprocesses

A great personal example for us is how we try to provide a meaningful learning experience. We don't just want to teach something. We want to create an experience that a student embraces and from which he or she walks away with more motivation, improved learning capabilities, and a passion for seeking out knowledge. To do that, we have to prepare for the experience, because it is not just about teaching.

In the following example, we use the ad-hoc subprocess to describe how we can prepare for the student experience. We are able to use the ad-hoc subprocess to illustrate four activities that we can do to prepare for that student experience. Ideally, we would want to complete all four activities. Using an ad-hoc subprocess, however, our process can continue after completing only one. The activities executed will be determined by the human performer—in this case, by us.

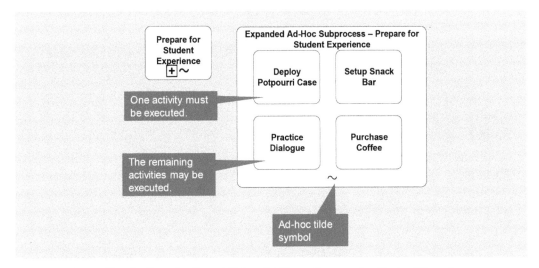

Figure 205: An Examination of Using Ad-Hoc—Prepare for Student Experience

There are other great uses for ad-hoc subprocesses. We see a significant use for ad-hoc subprocesses when multiple iterations could be executed, particularly in the IT world.

In the following example, we add an optional modeling technique that can be used for the ad-hoc expanded subprocess. While we depict four activities, we use a *sequence flow* between the first and second activity to represent a sequential process. We use *data associations* and *data objects* to represent *data dependencies*. The 32-bit version code and 64-bit version code are required to test the software code. We can implicitly model this for clarity.

So, depending on which activity the software developer executes (32 bits, 64 bits, or both), the subprocess begins. After producing the software version, the performer must test the software code. If the 32 bits is produced and tested, the subprocess could end using the ad-hoc notation. We are not required to test the 64-bit code; it is what occurs for that specific instantiation.

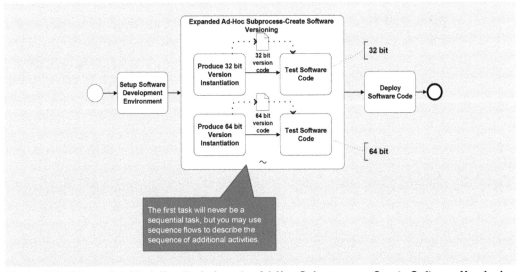

Figure 206: Alternative Modeling Technique for Ad-Hoc Subprocess—Create Software Versioning

General Practitioner
Using Ad Hoc Subprocesses for Business Process Improvement

I think the biggest thing that helps with the understanding is to practice modeling a fairly simple process using specific notations to make sure you could apply a principle.

Let's take the ad hoc expanded subprocess and practice modeling a simple process. Let's apply your ad-hoc knowledge to the following business process model for performing process improvement analysis. Use the following information to create an ad-hoc expanded subprocess.

There are two activities within the ad-hoc subprocess. The first produces multiple versions of business process models from a single business process model. Basically, we capture the *as-is* process as a baseline (the input to our ad-hoc expanded subprocess) and then create multiple versions of business process models to conduct *what-if* or *if-what* processes to analyze.

- Each iteration of the *to-be* process model development creates slightly different versions of the *to-be* state of the business process.
    - The three version types we create are:
        > A business process model to *automate* a process
        > A business process model that *outsources* our current process
        > A business process model that *improves* our process
- The second activity tests the output of the first activity. In this instance, *simulate the model.*
    - The iterations of the second activity are performed sequentially.
- The second activity, the simulation, starts as soon as each iteration of the first activity is completed.
    - Each version can be tested once a version of the *to-be* business process model is created.

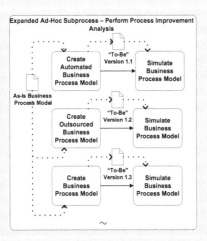

Figure 207: Perform Process Improvement Analysis—Ad-Hoc Solution

How did you model? Did you derive a different solution? If so, we would love if you shared it with us. Join our online discussion regarding ad hoc subprocesses.

We love seeing different modeling perspectives. While this is just one solution, there are many solutions. In fact, when building out this model, we discussed alternative ways to present the ad-hoc expanded subprocess solution.

Meditating Mike
Challenging How You Think in Action

Reflecting on previous experiences, imagining yourself in the third person, or watching yourself through a camera lens can be a powerful tool for examining how you act and react. Let's examine how negative influences can alter our behavior.

For this reflection exercise:

- Recall a previous modeling experience in which you had a negative experience (*it can be a learning experience with BPMN or a practitioner's experience when modeling with BPMN*).

- As you think about the specific negative experience, recall the following:

  – Who else was there?

  – What was the nature of the modeling experience?

  > Were you modeling with SMEs, fellow BPMN practitioners, or were you learning?

- Now think about the specific instance that had a negative impact on you.
    - Recall how you reacted physically. Did your heart rate rise? Did it increase your anxiety?
    - Recall how it made you feel. Sad? Angered? Confused? Embarrassed?
- As you think about this experience, identify and isolate what influence it had on the actions you took next.
    - Did you want to interact or become confrontational?
    - Did you break down and not react and not engage? Were you clear-headed?
- Now think about your action. How can you mitigate negative experiences that influence your actions?

4.1.5.5 BPMN Task Markers

In this section, we describe the remaining *task markers*. We have already seen one type of BPMN task marker in the previous section in the form of compensation. BPMN has three other types: the *loop* task marker, *parallel multi-instanced* marker, and *sequential multi-instance* marker. This section will dive into how you can effectively use these notations to bring a greater level of clarity to your business process models.

Figure 208: Illustration of Task Markers—Loop, Parallel, and Sequential

4.1.5.5.1 Loop Task Marker

The *loop task marker* is a great way to add context and illustrate when the same activity is completed multiple times. In essence, it saves us the trouble of creating the same activity over and over in our process model.

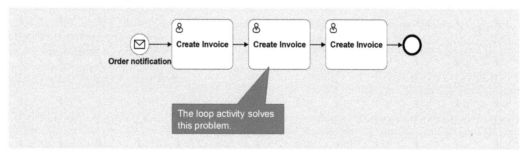

Figure 209: The Same Activity Over and Over

The loop task marker has several characteristics:

- Activity continues to occur while the loop condition is *true*, meaning the activity will be executed multiple times.
  - The loop task *instance attribute* is called a *loop counter*, meaning the activity executes the number of times (integer) the loop counter is set for.
- Depicted with a looped arrow
- Can be depicted with subprocess icon, which means it can be applied to *call*, *transaction*, *event*, or *normal* subprocesses
- Can be depicted with the compensation marker
- Can be depicted with an ad-hoc subprocess

In the following examples, we depict the loop activity in action. In the first example, we highlight how we *create invoices* until all of the orders are processed. We then validate those invoices until there are no more invoices to validate.

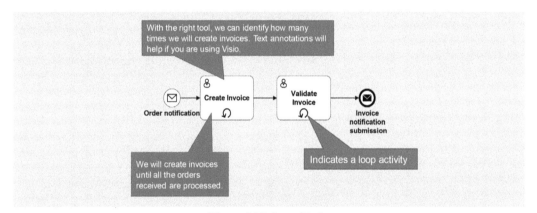

Figure 210: Loop Tasks

In the next example, we illustrate how we can apply text annotation to add context to the loop activity. Sometimes you are creating process models outside of a modeling tool capable of capturing the specific instances of the activity that will be run. Using text annotations is an alternative method for depicting that additional information.

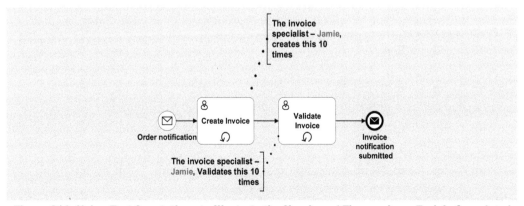

Figure 211: Using Text Annotations to Illustrate the Number of Times a Loop Task is Completed

Streamer Seth has created a video illustrating how we can use looping tasks for our system administrator's process.

Join us at https://www.bpmpractitioners.com/videos.

The videos match the figure name. You can also view our YouTube channel, *Joshua Fuehrer*.

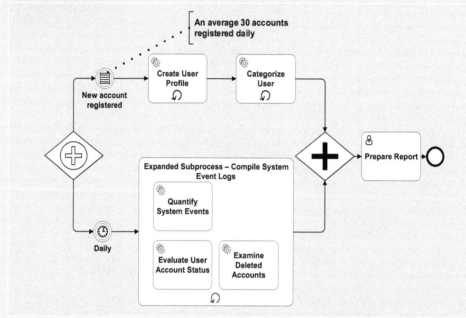

Figure 212: Streamer Seth Loop Task Video Example

4.1.5.5.2 Multi-Instance Markers

If you are like us, you have probably asked yourself, "What is the difference between the task loop markers and multi-instance markers?"

The key difference is that task loop markers represent activities that continue to occur, whereas *multi-instance markers* represent multiple instances of the same activity completed in parallel or sequentially.

The parallel multi-instanced task marker has several characteristics:

- Activity is performed *in parallel*, meaning multiple instances of the activity are executed and completed at the same time
- Depicted with three vertical lines
- Can be depicted with subprocess icon, which means it can be applied to *call*, *transaction*, *event*, or *normal* subprocesses
- Can be depicted with the compensation marker

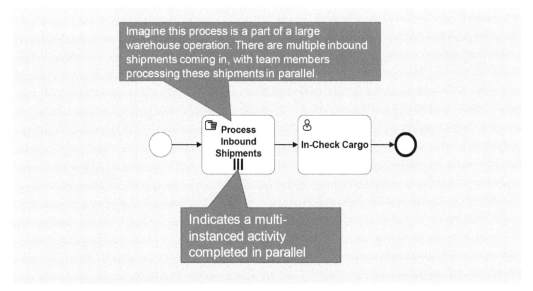

Figure 213: Using Multi-Instance Parallel Tasks—Shipment Processing

Yes and no. Yes, it is similar in that there is a sequential order in the task completion. Multi-instance tasks also have the *loop counter attribute*, meaning the activity executes the number of times (defined integer) the loop counter is set to.

The big difference between loop tasks and multi-instance tasks, however, is that there are *multiple instances* of the task being completed simultaneously or in parallel, meaning that the data input affects how the transformation of a multi-instanced task occurs.

For instance, each data input could affect how the transformation of activity occurs. Taking a look at the previous example for processing inbound shipments, one data input could be *general cargo*, another input could be *hazardous cargo*. While the processing of inbound shipments is completed in parallel, *the data input* would generate differences in the *time it would take* to process the inbound shipment. Basically, it takes longer, and there are more requirements for processing hazardous cargo.

BPMN also allows multi-instanced tasks to be completed sequentially. The *sequential multi-instanced task marker* has several characteristics:

- The activity is performed sequentially, meaning multiple instances of the activity are executed and completed in a specific order.

- Depicted with three horizontal lines

- Can be depicted with subprocess icon, which means they can be applied to *call*, *transaction*, *event*, or *normal* subprocesses

- Can be depicted with the compensation marker

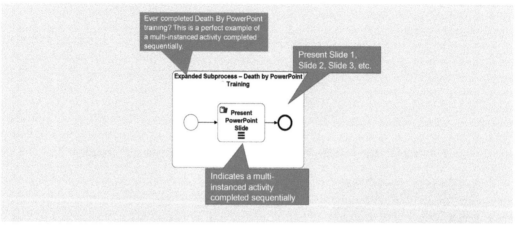

Figure 214: Death by PowerPoint Training—An Example of Multi-Instanced Sequential Activity

General Practitioner
Application of Multi-Instances Activities

Don't be afraid of failure: embrace it and use failure as a motivation to achieve anything.

Let's practice building a simple model using multi-instanced activities and explore how you could apply this notation when building business process models. In the following model, we describe tracking the movement of shipments. This is a common step in the logistics and transportation processes. A performer comes to work and throughout the day monitors the status of *multiple shipments*. We utilize the multiple events to highlight how various events can be the byproduct of the completion of each *monitor shipment* status. We show this as a parallel set of activities. We then can *record shipment status*, but we do this *sequentially* because we need to record the time of *each event*. We use the *sequential multi-instanced activity* to depict that we record the shipment status sequentially.

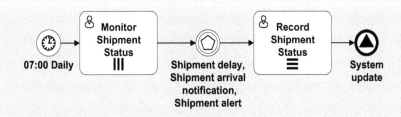

Figure 215: Developing a Basic Process Model with Multi-Instance Tasks

Surfer Dave Pro Tip

Whoa, dude. Do you think task markers mean I will keep shredding waves forever? It could, but in reality, the shredding would eventually end. That is some complex behavior there.

The key to remember is that multiple events can occur from the generation of multiple activities. For instance, each time I shred waves, various events could occur. Multiple events are thrown from the boundary of the activity, demonstrating that different states can occur during the execution of multi-instanced activities.

Meditating Mike
Examining How You Can Apply Knowledge in Your Organization

Take a moment and think about the processes within your organization. Can you think of where you could apply these notations to previously built models? But more importantly, can you think why it is important to update those models using the multi-instance task markers?

We find that the loop task marker, as well as the multi-instance markers, are useful when analyzing processes to streamline them. When we are trying to reduce process cycle time, understanding activities that have multi-instances or looping is critical for ensuring we depict resources used and the time the cycle takes. Because nothing would be worse than modeling out a process, capturing the metrics and resources, only to find out tasks are looping or multi-instanced. Imagine the differences you would see.

4.1.5.6 Modeling with the Remaining Task Types

In this section, we will define and then demonstrate how to apply the remaining task types. While some say we saved the best for last, we would say, we saved the most technical or most unused for last. Before you ask, we consider the *business rule task* and *script task* as the most complex but useful of the four remaining task types, whereas we typically don't see a lot of application for the *send* and *receive* tasks.

4.1.5.6.1 Business Rule Tasks

Business rule tasks are used to describe the business rules of our organizational processes. Business processes are filled with business rules. Rules govern how we operate and how our process works. Sometimes rules are explicitly defined and articulated through publications, operating manuals, or federal government regulations. Other times, business rules are the collection of working knowledge or *tacit knowledge* that employees use to optimize processes. These unspoken rules are not written down, but nevertheless, guide the actions taken.

In a way, employees' tacit knowledge can govern your organization's processes. To know how tacit knowledge governs your processes, you must surface employees' *mental models*. Surfacing employee mental models can occur during the interview process when creating process models. During the interview process, well-trained BPMN practitioners can uncover employee assumptions about how the process works, why employees react a certain way when an event occurs, or why, when, and how activities are completed.

The *business rule task* has several characteristics:

- Enables input and output to and from a *business rules engine*
- Depicted with a spreadsheet in the upper-left corner
- Same attributes as an activity
- When the task is executed, the business rules associated with the task are called.
- Can be depicted as a global business rule task

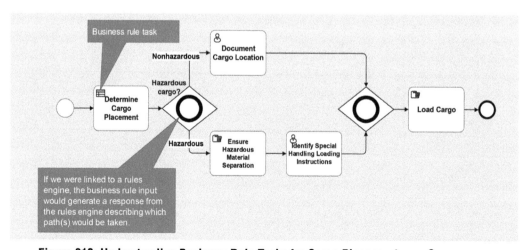

Figure 216: Understanding Business Rule Tasks for Cargo Placement on a Conveyance

Figure 217: Call Activity—Business Rule Task

General Practitioner
Application of Business Rules

I think as a matter of practice, people need to learn and continue to relearn. Looking at the problem from different viewpoints enables us to see patterns previously unsurfaced—the rules that govern science, truth, and how we are connected.

Let's analyze the following business process model and create a version of your own. In the following example, we describe the self-driving car. Obviously, current cars don't just automatically start driving (yet); first, the *autopilot* feature has to be engaged. As we continue down the road, sensors, along with the artificial intelligence (AI) unit, are *evaluating the road conditions*. Depending on the technical business rules (or written assumptions), one, two, or all three paths can be taken based on the data input and out from the business rule engine. For instance, the data input to the business rule engine could be *the speed of the car, the position of the car, current road conditions, the amount of traffic, the distance of the car in front or behind*, and so on. The output from the rules engine calculates (via AI in this instance) information to adjust the position of the car, speed, or continuous monitoring of the situation.

Now that we have presented the process, we want you to recreate this model. But this time, we want you to create another process path for a *business rule task* and *inclusive gateway*. Identify another possible adjustment an autonomous car could do.

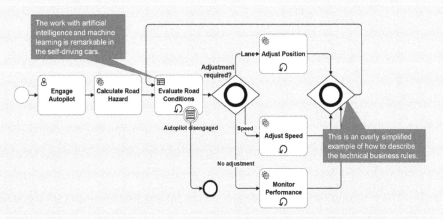

Figure 218: Analyzing the Technical Use of Business Tasks—Self-Driving Car Example

After you complete your model, join our business rule discussion on the forums and share your model.

Meditating Mike
Rules for Reflection

The most important step in improving your reflection is that you must make time to practice reflection. The more deeply you can examine the meaning behind your learning experience, the more likely you will surface true understanding that you couldn't see from the start.

Now that you have modeled with business rule tasks, particularly for a business rule, what comes to mind regarding the complexity of business rules? In a world of machine learning, AI, and advanced robotics, many of the old business rules of the past, like *each passenger must have a ticket*, seem so simplistic. How we account for and handle complexity is important as we starting using business process modeling for technical processes.

4.1.5.6.2 Script Tasks

In this section, we really dive into the technical nature of BPMN tasks with the introduction of *script tasks*. While we covered service tasks in chapter 3, script tasks are an alternative for modeling out technical tasks. Script tasks are used by a *process engine*, so as you think about how you can use script tasks, think about things like *reporting tasks* or *automatic email processing tasks*. Another example of a script task in action is when a script accesses and invokes a *pull* of usernames from an active directory service. The pattern between all three descriptions here is that script tasks are invoking scripts.

The script task has several characteristics:

- Executed by a business process engine
  - When the task is started, the engine will execute the script.
- Depicted as a wavy paper in the upper-left corner
- Upon activation, the script is invoked
- Same attributes as an activity

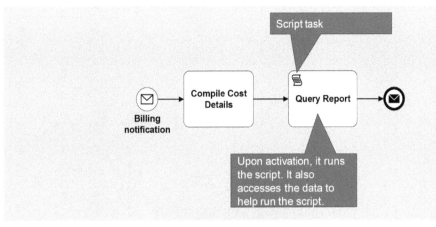

Figure 219: Script Tasks

Figure 220: Call Activity—Script Task

General Practitioner
Script Task Practice Session

Did you guess that many of my quotes about action came from transcripts of interviews with previous participants and peer review sessions? This was a method for sharing other BPMN practitioners' views in a fun and engaging way. I hope you have enjoyed them.

While we don't expect everyone to start out modeling script tasks, we do imagine at some point, when modeling in your organization, you will come across script tasks. The following model describes a business model for receiving an email. For this example, we just want you to recreate the model.

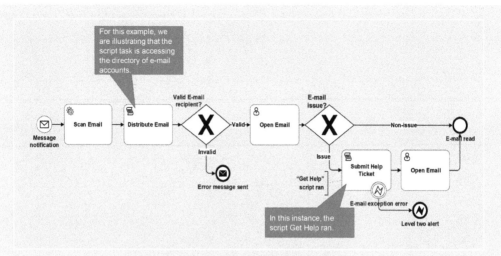

Figure 221: Applying Script Tasks

We used a text annotation to illustrate the script name that is running for the *submit help ticket* task, mainly because in our example we chose not to use any particular modeling tool, so using text annotation adds context to the model. The context can be valuable to technical experts as we call out the specific script name. If we moved into a modeling tool environment, we would have specific details associated with the script task (represented in the text annotation) that would enable successful simulation because we were able to invoke the correct script.

Forum Felicia
Making Meaningful Connections with BPMN Practitioners

Join the discussion on business rule tasks and script tasks. The following discussion provides some other practitioners view on the application of script, business rule, and service tasks.

Connecting with colleagues not only makes great connections in the BPMN community but also facilitates the transfer of BPMN knowledge. We encourage you to try to add a response to the user forum post based on your understanding of any one of these notations. It is always good to share your interpretation and collaborate with other practitioners to form a shared understanding of the notations. Who knows? By building connections, you may form lasting BPMN connections and expand your professional network:

https://groups.google.com/forum/#!topic/BPMNforum/kcRJhKafw9s

4.1.5.6.3 Receive Task and Receive Instantiating Task

The *receive task* is just as it sounds: It receives messages. To be more specific, it receives messages from *participants*. We will discuss two variations of the receive task. The first is the typical receive task; the second is the receive task that can instantiate a process.

The *receive task* has several characteristics:

- Requires a *message* to complete the task
- Depicted with an envelope in the upper-left corner
- Received from an *external participant*
- Can use *message flow* to connect receive task
- Can be used as an event-based gateway

Figure 222: Receive Task

By contrast, the receive task that *instantiates a process* has the following characteristics:

- Instantiate attribute set to *true*
- Depicted with a message start event in the upper-left corner
- Does not use a start event or incoming sequence flows

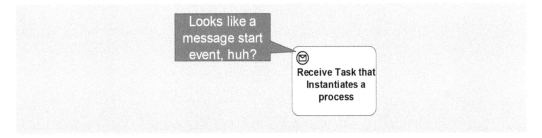

Figure 223: Receive Task that Instantiates a Process

There are a few examples worth mentioning regarding receive tasks and receive tasks that instantiate a process. In the following examples, we illustrate how and when you would apply them. To do this, we use one of our favorite processes for this: the invoicing and payment process.

In the following example, when an *order is received*, we must *submit an invoice*. Here is where we can expand our understanding of receive tasks and event-based gateways—specifically, the application of receive tasks after an event-based gateway.

We use the *receive task* to illustrate that when a payment is received, that processing path is taken. (As a reminder, event-based gateways only allow for one path to be taken, so the first triggered event, or in this case, receive task, continues the process. The process doesn't wait for the timer event *72 hours* in this instance.) Another important concept with the receive task is how it handles data. Specifically, when data is received, the receive task assigns a *data output* which is available to the process.

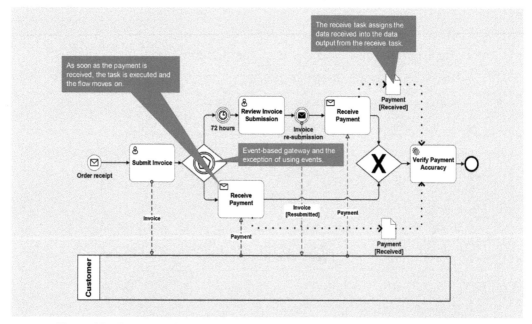

Figure 224: Interpretation of Receive Task and Event-based Gateway Application

Meditating Mike
Observing BPMN Patterns

Wait a minute. Take a moment and take a closer look at the start event order receipt *in the previous model. Didn't you just tell us that a receive task can instantiate a process when a message is received?*

That is a very keen observation. An alternative way to model the previous example is illustrated in the next figure. The key change is that we replace the message start event with a *receive task that instantiates a process*. The other key change is that there is no inbound sequence flow into the task.

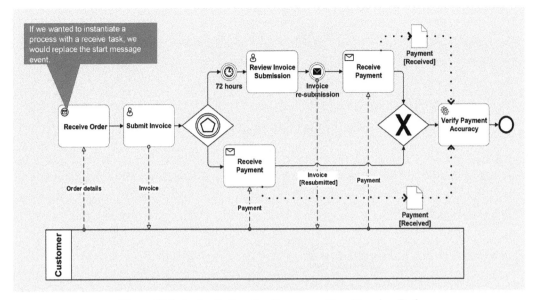

Figure 225: Instantiating the Process with a Receive Task

We have seen various uses for receive tasks, and specifically their naming conventions. We stick with the verb-subject style but have found interesting ways to illustrate *message received*. For example, we can receive all kinds of messages, so we could see all kinds of messages for receive tasks. The following are a few examples we have seen.

Figure 226: Receive Task Naming Conventions from other BPMN Practitioners

4.1.5.6.4 Send Tasks

The previous section described receive tasks. As you probably guessed from the title of this section, here we describe *send tasks*. Specifically, we will illustrate how you can use send tasks when developing your business process models.

Let's describe send task characteristics first.

- Requires a message to be sent to complete the task
- Depicted with a dark-filled envelope in the upper-left corner
- Sent to an external participant

Figure 227: Send Task

In essence, the send task is just the opposite of the receive task in that, instead of receiving messages and providing data to the process, the send task *takes data* from the process and *sends* that data out of the process to external participants. Let's demonstrate this in action in the following example.

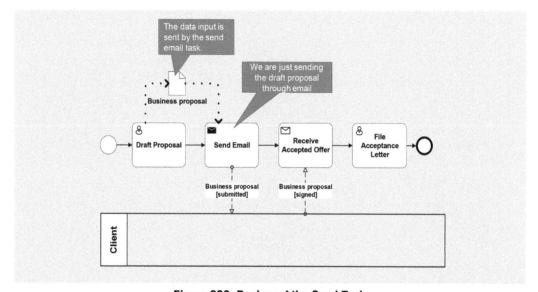

Figure 228: Review of the Send Task

Wait a second. I can extrapolate a pattern here with send and receive tasks. It's—hmmm…a lot like throw and catch message events.

That is correct. We can deduce that pattern as well by looking at the *message throw and catch* concept. We typically use message throw and catch events to depict this. However, some BPMN practitioners like to use the *send and receive tasks,* as they allow for exceptions and enable boundary events to be placed on the activity.

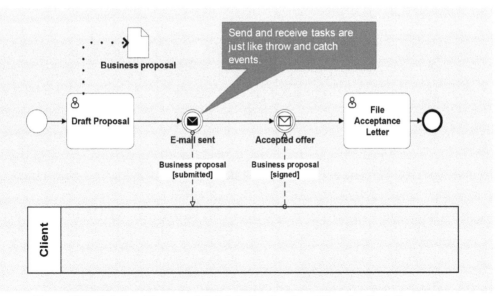

Figure 229: Relating Throw and Catch to the Send and Receive Task Concepts

General Practitioner
Experience with Send and Receive Tasks

Let's practice building with send and receive tasks. Some-times it just takes practice and reflection to determine the applicability of the notation for your organization.

Let's experiment modeling with send and receive tasks in the following investigation process. (For the sake of simplicity for the book, we excluded the participant pool.)

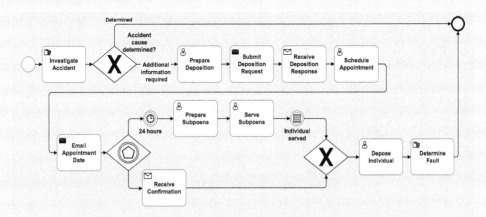

Figure 230: Experiment Modeling with Send and Receive Tasks

Meditating Mike
Using Previous Experience to Do It Differently

Building one way may seem great. How do you determine what notations to use? Is there a method to your approach? Take a moment and think how you would model the previous example differently.

As you were building out the model, how many of you thought about using *message throw and catches*? In the following example, we thought about how we could model the process differently and updated our model.

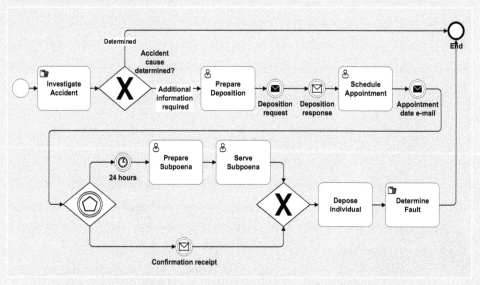

Figure 231: Reflection is the Key—Example of Simplifying a Model

Surfer Dave Pro Tip

OK. To make this simple, use message tasks only when the message can be interrupted.

This pro tip will save you time and energy when trying to decide, "Should I or should I not use message tasks?"

4.1.6 Learning BPMN as a Team

In this section, we engage those looking for a challenge in a thought experiment. This challenge is not for the faint of heart. It is for those truly committed to expanding their understanding of BPMN and applying it.

Don't worry no one can possibly know everything. The main point of the thought experiment is to get you to challenge your understanding and see things from another team member's perspective.

The interpretation of BPMN is by and large from our own viewpoints. Meaning, as we learn and apply the specification based on our comprehension of the modeling language syntax and semantics, we form individual viewpoints, which are subjective. This book is written from the authors' unique viewpoints and comprehension of BPMN. Even as a team, we had lengthy discussions about how best to teach concepts based on our understanding of a notation. We hope that those who truly excel in learning BPMN see *better* ways to model and teach certain concepts and provide that feedback, and we are ready and willing to listen to your viewpoints.

A key point: viewpoints formed based on ambiguous or unclear guidance only adds to the complexity of learning and modeling with BPMN. Ambiguous examples or ambiguous situations require teams to solve complex modeling problems to avoid costly mistakes for an organization.

Let's examine the following thought experiment.

Thought Experiment Introduction

Take a moment and imagine you are given the opportunity to work with a famous colleague, theorist, or practitioner.

Corporate leadership brought you in for a meeting at 4:00 p.m. and introduces you to this famous individual. They notify you that you will be working together to solve a complex problem in the field using BPMN. They believe that by working together, you can not only solve this complex problem but also apply the methodology to solve complex organizational problems and bring a new level of competitive advantage previously unrealized in your company.

The famous colleague, theorist, or practitioner is excited to be working with you and very eager to learn about BPMN so that person can understand your work. However, corporate leadership states that you will only have three hours together before a 7:00 p.m. flight.

Now sit back and think about this situation. If you had someone who is primed for learning and eager to learn as much as possible in three hours, what would you teach?

Specifically, identify:

1. The *process* you would lay out to teach the person

2. What you think is *critical* to share with the person for learning BPMN

To achieve this goal, we want you to find a *group* of colleagues to complete this thought experiment.

There are several ways to do this. If you are process modeling in an organization, seek out colleagues who are using or learning BPMN, or go to our BPMN thought experiment forum page and post that you are looking to collaborate on this experience.

Once you have your group (at least three people), share this exercise with them. You can download this thought experiment from our thought experiment resource page or share this book with group members.

After everyone in the group has reflected on those questions, as a group:

1. Create a model of the notations you would use as a legend.

2. Create a slide describing your team's collective knowledge regarding how you would teach the person in three hours.

   a. Where would you start?

   b. What concepts would you include?

   c. How would you make those three hours meaningful?

As individuals share their views on why they think a specific notation should be covered, try to add to their comments in a meaningful way.

For example, when someone states the importance of exclusive gateways, the following is an example of how you could respond:

- Initial response: "I concur," or, "I have not thought of that description from that perspective/viewpoint before."

- Add-on: "I wonder: have you thought about the nature of data-based gateways and that the data generated from the previous activity determines the path the token transverses?"

The best part of this thought experiment is that we don't expect everyone to be an expert or to have a complex understanding of each notation. That's OK. The idea is that when you are unfamiliar or unsure of a notation, and someone else states they don't know or don't fully understand, this gives you an opportunity to discuss it further and expand your understanding.

When you finish your team's model and slide, post it on the forums. We would love to hear from BPMN practitioners like yourself.

4.2 Closing View

This chapter expanded on BPMN to include the remaining notations and how you can apply these to your business process models. This chapter intended to firmly establish a framework for modeling syntactically correct models.

If we were successful, the next chapter will enable you to take on a practitioner mindset. We will share our experiences with BPMN in a real-world enterprise, illustrate how we used

BPMN models to inform BPM initiatives and highlight how BPMN models can be used with other types of methodologies and frameworks.

Lastly, take time to reflect on the goals you set when you were going through chapter 4. Ask yourself, did you see benefits from setting specific learning goals? Was your goal well formulated, so you were able to plan and see the impact of your goal as it relates to understanding BPMN? More importantly, did your goal increase/improve the *desired outcome* that you set?

Please join our goal-setting group on our forum section and let's discuss your journey.

5. Real-World BPMN for the Practitioner

5.1   Areas for Application

We hope we have provided a learning experience so far that you have valued and has been meaningful. In this chapter, we are going to share how you can go from process documentation with BPMN to the application of BPMN through various approaches. With our unique backgrounds and consulting experiences, we have been exposed to multiple organizations that have applied different frameworks or approaches using BPMN to achieve specific outcomes. This chapter provides us the opportunity to share strategies for applying BPMN to various BPM initiatives.

5.1.1   Leveraging BPMN Models for Organization Initiatives

Many of you are a part of organizations that have started or are in the middle of BPM initiatives and are already using BPMN to model out organizational processes. In fact, many of you probably have 50 percent or more of your organizational business processes modeled out if you have been underway for a while. Getting to that 50 percent mark, you probably began to see the light at the end of the tunnel. As you start to see the light, though, questions probably surfaced regarding your process documentation efforts.

A common question we have heard as advisors is, "How do we move from process documentation into practical application and process improvement?"

It's a great question, and in this section, we dive into the practical application of BPMN.

5.1.1.1   Application of BPMN with Lean Six Sigma and the Define, Measure, Analyze, Improve, and Control (DMAIC) Quality Improvement Process

A thing we hear a lot from BPMN practitioners is, "How can BPMN be used to complement process improvement techniques such as Lean Six Sigma?"

We would like to share our experiences regarding how your business process modeling efforts can link directly into the Lean Six Sigma Define, Measure, Analyze, Improve, and Control (DMAIC) quality improvement process. An organization modeling effort can tie directly into many areas of DMAIC. For instance, in organizations that already have their as-is processes modeled, those same BPMN models can be:

1. Used to help define *customers* and their *requirements*

2. Used to help identify *opportunities for improvement*

Business process models provide a framework for extracting pertinent details required to help define the problem and develop your project charter. Specifically, when BPMN models are capturing process details and the tacit knowledge of an organization's workforce, you can leverage previous modeling efforts to define known problems.

In the following example, we lay out a process for dry cleaning; specifically, a service that some dry cleaners provide, which is delivery and pickup of dry-cleaned goods. During our previous modeling of the operational process, we captured key information based on feedback from delivery drivers. Two key problem areas they identified were that, while all customers receive a phone call reminding them to set out their dry cleaning, customers do not always have dry cleaning to pick up. Likewise, while some customers aren't receiving any dry cleaning, the driver still arrives at the customer's location.

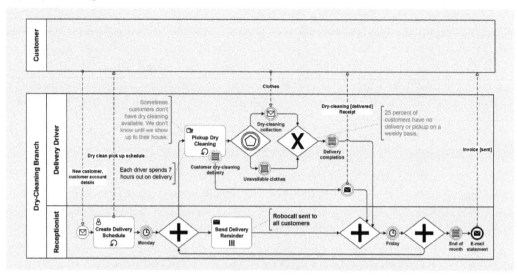

Figure 232: Analyzing BPMN Models to Define a Problem

Analyzing already-developed business process models enables you to create a framework for defining a problem statement. The following is a framework for crafting the problem statement answering the five *W*s based on the previous dry-cleaning business process model:

> Dry cleaning *delivery drivers* are spending two unnecessary hours out on delivery routes each week due to customers not having a dry-cleaning requirement. The company is spending resources on gas, maintenance of the fleet, and employee salaries for services that are not always required. The dry-cleaning business failed to implement a robocall program to improve the delivery service provided.

Now that we have used our BPMN to *help define the problem,* we can use the BPMN model to identify benchmarked *process times and metrics* relevant to your organization. Measuring baselines is essential for determining priorities to improve the quality of your processes or the quality of the service your organization provides.

Measuring requires establishing current baselines as the basis for improvement. Therefore, business process models that capture activities' metrics and benchmarked processing time will have a considerable advantage when moving into the measuring phase of the DMIAC process.

Let's expand on the previous example a bit. In the following example, we look at the captured metrics in which 25 percent of the time, no customers have a weekly pickup or delivery. From that data, we can quantify the drive time, costs related to that extra driving, wasted opportunity costs, and so on. It's all about the level of detail that you are capturing when developing business process models. It's vital that models capture *processing time* for activities, any *lag time*, and specific metrics related to the process, such as 25 percent of the customers do not have a pickup or delivery on a weekly basis. Doing so enables BPMN practitioners to measure the baselines and perform additional analysis.

We have found that by analyzing business process models, we can pull critical pieces of data required for the third step of the DMIAC process—analyze. Analyzing business processes will enable you to quickly organize the business and system process opportunities and prioritize known problems. Specifically, when your business processes highlight known issues, gaps, and opportunities, you will have a jump start for root cause analysis. In the following example, we pinpoint a potential problem area and start analyzing known datasets within the process and within the organization.

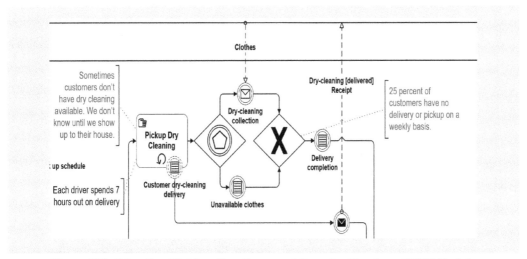

Figure 233: Extracting Metrics, Baselines, and Opportunities from BPMN Models

Improving organizational business process problems is often what we are called to do as business process analysts. We love to see positive change. We love that we can be the catalyst for promoting positive change. Developing *to-be* BPMN models enables the testing of *to-be* solutions before we execute change. It's doing the *what-if* or *if-what* drill. In fact, doing *to-be* BPMN models is a practice we encourage when developing organizational business process models that have known gaps, problem areas, or opportunities identified by SMEs.

We examined why the robocall system failed and used that analysis to create a *to-be* process to improve the effectiveness of our processes as well as to create a strategy to ensure success while mitigating costs.

In the following example, we describe a *to-be* solution through the development of an application that customers can use to confirm pickup with the press of a button. We also describe how GPS route profiles are updated when customers confirm they require no pickup; if customers do not have a drop-off or pick-up scheduled, the driver's route profile is updated, and the route is updated.

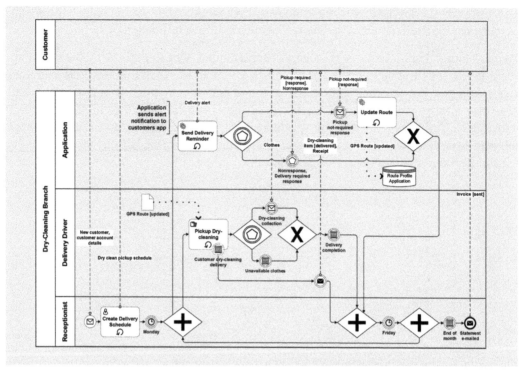

Figure 234: To-Be or Not To-Be—What-If Business Process Model

One thing not listed on the BPMN model but considered in the analysis of the *to-be* model was a modification to the customer agreement. By thinking of the *what-ifs*, we identified that we needed to update the customer agreement, incentivizing the use of the application. When customers use the app to notify for delivery or non-delivery, they receive a discounted rate on their monthly statement. That discounted rate is offset by the resources saved in salaries, maintenance, and fuel costs.

While we don't create *to-be* models for every organizational process (nor would we advocate for that because of the resources required to undertake such an effort), we do find it extremely beneficial when *to-be* BPMN models are readily available when a DMAIC quality improvement process begins. If you don't have the *to-be* modeled, however, don't fret. Using the *as-is* BPMN model as a baseline provides a stepping stone into the *to-be* development phase for improving the business process.

5.1.1.2 Applying BPMN to the Internet of Things (IoT)

The Internet of Things (IoT) is another exciting area for the application of BPMN models. IoT has exploded in recent years and can have a tremendous impact on organizational processes—mainly when trying to develop the *to-be* state of your organizational processes.

Hospital processes have been a keen area of interest for the application of BPMN efforts, particularly as they relate to the IoT. Static *as-is* processes of tomorrow offer a glut of opportunity for business and technical analysts as they begin to extract up-to-date information. Take, for example, the process of the Emergency Management System (EMS)

Dispatch Call Center. On the surface, it seems like a straightforward process, with phone calls, radios, computers, and the network devices to support those enabling the success of the process.

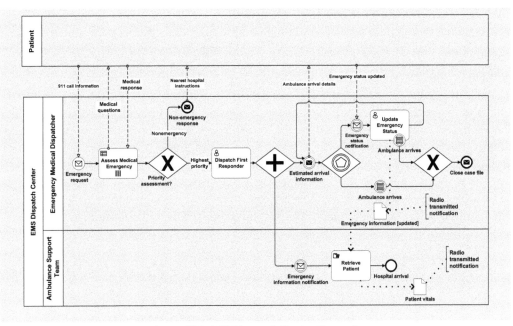

Figure 235: IoT Dispatch Center Example

Several hospitals have embarked on embracing process improvement through the adoption of technological implementations through IoT. Before we dive into some reflection questions, for those who are unaware, leveraging BPMN process models is fundamental for IoT architectures. In fact, IoT and BPMN go hand in hand, because embedded within the processes are technologies that, when harnessed, are very important to an IoT architecture. The following is a small subset of IoT devices for the EMS Dispatch Center process.

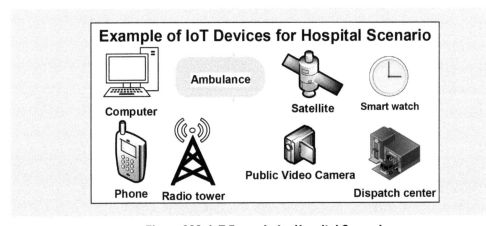

Figure 236: IoT Example for Hospital Scenario

Also within the realm of the IoT architecture are all the networks required to support these devices. While we don't capture those specific networks in the process models, we do capture one fundamental concept needed for building out your IoT architecture: the data.

Take, for example, the previous EMS Dispatch Center process. Take a minute and ask yourself *what type of data* could be documented for analysis in the process model. Notably, as a business analyst or modeler, what can you identify that would help provide decision support for hospital leadership as it relates to their complex business processes?

The following is an example of how you can use BPMN with your IoT architecture to identify critical components for analysis. For instance, we use the EMS system database and GPS database, two *as-is* systems that enable the transformation of the depicted business process. The GPS database provides real-time traffic reports and quickest routes for the dispatcher and ambulance support team. For instance, if a traffic jam occurs, the GPS database will provide updated routes for the ambulance driver. It is important when documenting these IoT business processes to note what technology and data are already in place and what are not. Doing so will enable you to identify opportunities when developing your *to-be* processes.

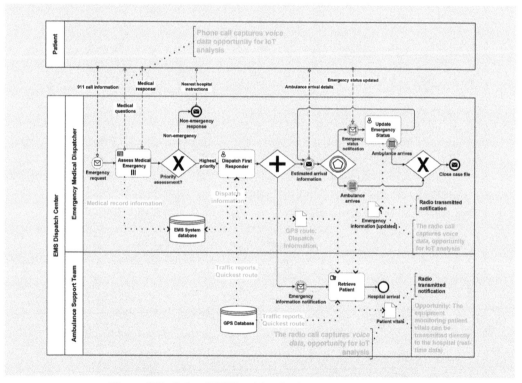

Figure 237: Using BPMN to Identify IoT Devices and Data

Let us show you an example of capturing opportunities for our *to-be* process. In the previous example, we identified an opportunity to capture cell phone *voice data* within our *as-is* process. In the IoT, voice data, camera data, satellite data, system data, and so on are all important considerations when trying to analyze and improve business processes. For instance, patient vitals (system data) provide an opportunity for change in our *to-be* process *if* the equipment used to monitor the patient can upload the data via the system and transmit it via satellite to the hospital directly. This *what-if* change could have a significant impact on the start of the next process at the hospital.

Think of it this way: Anything that can be connected to the internet can be connected to the cloud, and the resulting data can be examined. Things we usually wouldn't think of as connected are now connected or have the potential to be connected. As these connections become more explicit, you will begin to see patterns, similar to process modeling.

5.1.1.3 Shaping *To-Be* System Requirements

As enterprise architects, we are always expanding the application of EA knowledge. Creating actionable knowledge with our enterprise assets (EA artifacts, primitives, and captured tacit knowledge) is essential for linking operational processes and capability with the IT solutions we rely on.

If we had to focus on one area of this book, it would be a modernization of legacy systems. A lot of organizations today are still filled with legacy systems or legacy processes which rely heavily on manual actions and aging systems. These legacy systems significantly reduce the competitive advantage potential of an organization, which to us provides the biggest opportunity to capture the *as-is* state and the steps organization members complete to help shape the *to-be* system requirements to modernize an organization's aging systems and legacy processes.

Let's examine the following process model, in which we examine a legacy process using a combination of commercial tools and a legacy system. For this *as-is*, you will notice we use the account manager in the pool. The account manager perspective is the key focus, as we identified key problem areas during our high-level analysis. We created a drill-down perspective using BPMN. So, this is a little different than you might be used to seeing. In the example, we represent two lanes as tools: the commercial tool user interface and account module user interface. We are doing so to illustrate a significant problem in our legacy process. This technique allows us to describe the unique steps for each tool and to highlight our reliance on the commercial tool and issues that currently exist.

As you will see, to get a report, we must request it in the commercial tool. Additionally, we must wait for the commercial tool automation to provide the report. Once the account manager receives the report, he or she must manually review the report's accuracy. Even though the account manager has access to the report in the legacy system, determining the accuracy of the report occurs *outside* of the system. It's important for the organization to identify these manual steps in the legacy process because, in an earlier company study, it was determined that the account manager spends twenty hours a month manually reviewing reports and completing them outside of any known system.

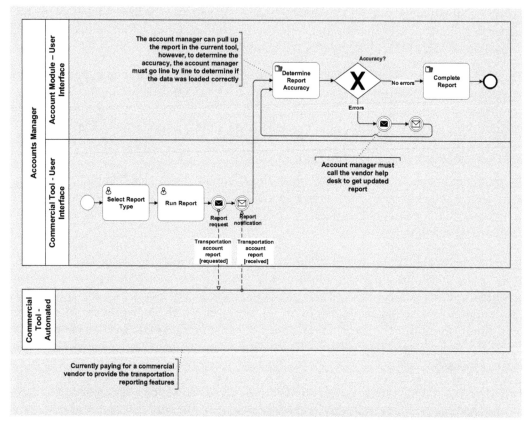

Figure 238: As-Is Legacy Process and Legacy System Business Process Model

We are in luck, however, with BPMN. We can use this *as-is* model as our baseline to create a *to-be* version to help identify new system requirements. While the BPMN model won't provide all the details needed to hire a vendor or put software developers to work, it will provide the necessary information to illustrate what we expect our *to-be* state to look like *and* how it will reduce our process time by eliminating current manual actions.

As you can see in the following model, we remove the commercial tool and update our application to account for key features and automation. We now need to improve our processes and the accuracy of our reports.

Ask yourself this: What else could we have added to our *to-be* model?

Our answers: We could have added data requirements to give it that extra detail, or text annotations to shape our expected runtime or activity processing time.

Did you think of something else? Join our discussion on the forums and share your insights.

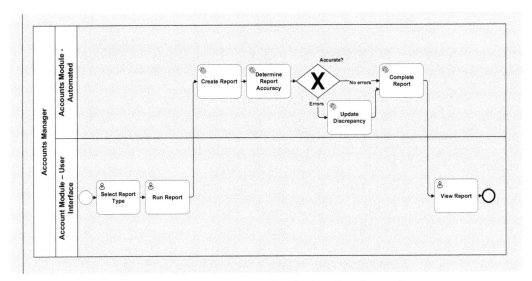

Figure 239: To-Be Automation System Requirement

Like many of you, we love to be able to leverage our BPMN models for various efforts. While the list we presented is not all-encompassing, it does provide some insights you may find useful in a few areas.

5.2 Your Organization's Role in Applying Success Factors for BPM Initiatives

We wanted to conclude this section with a discussion of essential considerations for modeling with BPMN. Specifically, we wanted to identify critical steps required for successful BPM initiatives using BPMN. The reason is many organizations that have implemented BPMN have various levels of commitment and support. During our research and engagement with customers, we have identified some key success factors you can use and help instill in your organization.

Business process modeling notation key success factors reflect: (1) a set of organizational functions, (2) learning mode activities that influence the creation of knowledge, and (3) best practices for the application of business process modeling activities that affect the development of business process models. We group key success factors into three categories: management support, support for learning, and effective approaches for BPMN acceptance.

5.2.1 Management Support

Let's start with an important consideration that will make or break successful BPM initiatives, learning BPMN, and any effective approach to encouraging BPMN acceptance. That consideration is support from management.

Management support is vital. Through management support, modeling efforts can occur and flourish. Why? Because you will have access to the organizational processes and members in those processes you are trying to model out. Those who share the vision of leadership for BPM initiatives will see the power of business process improvement, redesign, or reengineering.

We have seen how management support improves collaborative modeling efforts and the peer-review process for developing business process models. Additionally, when leaders promote an environment for training at all levels, the development of business process models is more successful.

It is also very important for management to provide the resources to purchase modeling tools for learning BPMN and supporting BPM initiatives. Good modeling tools that have built-in syntax checkers, animation features, and simulation capabilities have a positive influence on learning BPMN. They help reinforce good modeling practices. These tools also reinforce what BPMN practitioners learn. We are not saying that good modeling tools will teach you BPMN, but they do help—especially when you combine various learning modes and then are able to apply those concepts in a good modeling tool.

Conversely, a lack of management support is detrimental not only to learning but to the application of BPMN for modeling efforts. Take, for example, when management does not perceive the value of business process modeling. We have observed when management lacks such perception, you are less likely to have access to SMEs and less likely to get feedback to validate the process models you are developing. Worse yet, when you do get feedback, you tend to get a hand wave from leadership saying, "Yep, that looks good."

5.2.2 Support for Learning

Let's take a moment and take a more in-depth look at the support for learning. Probably the most critical aspect of learning BPMN is to *avoid learning by yourself*. Just as management support for BPM initiatives is essential, management that embraces a *learning organization mindset* is vital.

Organizations that support learning through trainers, coaches, and mentors who are practitioners of BPMN will influence the understanding and application of BPMN. The key when bringing in trainers is that they are practitioners of BPMN, *not just teachers*. Trainers who are practitioners influence the understanding of BPMN through in-depth training. They can answer questions on the fly. They also provide learning experiences that relate to the organization's processes because they know the value of making meaningful connections. Because in the end, if you are a supply chain company, and you try to teach BPMN using a cookie-cutter approach, chances are learning just won't be as effective.

The importance of interactions among experts in the organization is a crucial component for developing BPMN understanding and applying it effectively to modeling efforts. The peer-review process influences the understanding of BPMN and affects the model development process through interactions with experts. The peer-review process is an aspect often overlooked in organizations. Just as in scientific or business journals, peer review is a cornerstone for publication of high-quality papers. The same concept applies to BPMN. By having a peer-review process, you can improve the learning of BPMN and the quality of your business process models. We have formed a team of dedicated peer-review experts who provide model validation, modeling recommendations, and Q&A sessions.

5.2.3 Effective Approaches for Teaching BPMN and Applying it to Organizational Modeling Efforts

At this point we're sure that many of you will attest to the complexity of BPMN, and nontechnical users will find it even more complex. In our experience, the more complex or technical something is, the more likely nontechnical users avoid it like the plague. They may take a look and say, "Yep, that's my process," without trying to understand what you have modeled. They may just avoid you.

But by using your knowledge about your organization's processes and what you have learned in this book, you can apply some techniques to improve the acceptability of BPMN while enhancing the understanding of BPMN for nontechnical users.

The first approach you can apply is looking at the modeling notation subset you are using. Using every notation is not really useful, as nontechnical users will become quickly overwhelmed. But if you take the time to develop a simple legend explaining the basic notations in a way that relates to your organization's processes, you can remove the fear of not knowing, or at least mitigate it.

This means taking time in your organization with other BPMN practitioners, examining what that BPMN legend would look like, and thinking about how you can describe the notations in a way that resonates with readers. Doing so will enable you to make connections with those readers, and over time build up their basic understanding of BPMN. Additionally, it will also allow those nontechnical experts to really see themselves in the business process models you are developing. In the end, if those nontechnical users become advocates of your work, you will have a higher chance of success as you continue modeling out your organizational processes.

We created a legend for clients in the past and posted a copy on our website; feel free to use this as your baseline and modify it as fits your organizational process needs). You will notice we moved away from some of the BPMN language and tailored it for a specific business audience.

The second approach we have found useful is keeping it simple. Not just in the notations we use for the first round of modeling, but also in how we model. We focus on keeping it simple by capturing the happy-day process. Doing so, we can keep the client or expert engaged in what typically occurs and teach them the basics of a normal business process flow. Expanding after that first modeling session is critical to ensure you don't fall into the trap of misusing BPMN for the sake of always keeping it simple.

6. Conclusion

We found it hard to end this book. "Why?" you might be asking. Basically, we wanted to provide you with more learning experiences and enhance the skills you have acquired during this learning experience. For us, learning never ends. For you, learning never ends. If you have been engaging in practice and reflection, you are well on your way, but *don't stop with this book.*

We hope that you are ready to continue your journey with BPMN. There are pockets of great resources out there. The key for you, just like other BPMN practitioners, is to harness those resources to learn and apply BPMN effectively.

To help you continue your adult learning journey with BPMN, we have created a one-stop shop for training material, videos, and interactive discussions. We encourage you and those in your organization to join us. Share your experiences. Share your process for learning. Share your struggles. Together, we can learn BPMN and think of new and exciting ways to depict our organizational process models.

Join us at www.bpmpractitioners.com

7. Bibliography

Boggs, Jason Bruce, Jillian Lane Cohen, and Gwen C. Marchand. "The Effects of Doodling on Recall Ability." *Psychological Thought*. March 31, 2017. doi:10.1037/e610222013-001.

Fuehrer, Joshua G. "Learning Approaches That Influence Business Process Modeling and Notation: A Generic Qualitative Inquiry." Ph.D. diss., Cappella University, 2017.

Google BPMN Forum. Retrieved from https://groups.google.com/forum/#!forum/bpmnforum

David A. Kolb, *Experiential Learning: Experience as the Source of Learning and Development*, Upper Saddle River, NJ: Pearson Education, 2015.

Leopold, Henrik, Jan Mendling, and Oliver Gunther. "What We Can Learn from Quality Issues of BPMN Models from Industry." *IEEE Software*. March 2015. https://www.computer.org/csdl/mags/so/preprint/07106381.html doi:10.1109/MS.2015.81

"Business Process Model & Notation (BPMN)." *About the Common Object Request Broker Architecture Specification* Accessed May 14, 2018. http://www.omg.org/bpmn/index.htm.

"Object Management Group Business Process Model and Notation." *Object Management Group BPMN Specification.* Accessed May 14, 2018. http://www.bpmn.org/.

Recker, J. (2010). "Opportunities and constraints: The current struggle with BPMN". *Business Process Management Journal*, 16, 181-201. doi:10.1108/14637151011018001

Senge, Peter M. *The Fifth Discipline: The Art and Practice of the Learning Organization*. New York: Doubleday, 1990.

Suman, R. A., Sajeev, B S., & Ranjan, A. (2014). "An empirical study of error patterns in industrial business process models". *IEEE Transactions on Services Computing*, 7, 140-153. doi:10.1109/TSC.2013.10

Trisotech. All Trisotech Models. Retrieved from www.Trisotech.com